PUREBRED RESCUE DOG ADOPTION

ALSO BY LIZ PALIKA FROM HOWELL BOOK HOUSE:

All Dogs Need Some Training

The Australian Shepherd: Champion of Versatility

The Australian Shepherd: An Owner's Guide to a Happy Healthy Pet

The German Shepherd Dog: An Owner's Guide to a Happy Healthy Pet

PUREBRED RESCUE DOG ADOPTION

....

REWARDS AND REALITIES

Liz Palika

HOWELL
BOOK
HOUSE

Library of Congress Cataloging-in-Publication Data
Palika, Liz, date.
   Purebred rescue dog adoption: rewards and realities/Liz Palika.
     p. cm.
   ISBN 0-7645-4971-5 (alk. paper)
1. Rescue dogs. 2. Dog adoption. I. Title.
SF428.55.P35 2004
636.73—dc22   2003016101

Manufactured in the United States of America

10 9 8 7 6 5 4 3 2 1

CONTENTS

INTRODUCTION

Watachie was a purebred rescue dog. He and his littermates had been abandoned in a rural area and survived by eating road kill. The four surviving puppies (at least three had been hit by cars) were taken in by German Shepherd Dog Rescue, as the puppies appeared to be German Shepherds and, to be honest, one of the group's volunteers had a soft spot for puppies! Infested with internal parasites, suffering from bronchitis, skinny and wary of people, the puppies were not in the best of shape. I adopted one of them only after the rescue volunteers warned me of the special care he would need.

As he grew, it became very clear that he was, indeed, a purebred German Shepherd. He was handsome, quick thinking, funny and wanted to please me. He thrived in obedience training, competed in Frisbee contests, learned to pull a wagon and learned agility on a police dog obstacle course. He became a certified search and rescue dog, and with an AKC ILP (Indefinite Listing Privilege), earned his Utility Dog title with several High in Trials and High Combined Scores.

Even though I had owned dogs before, I had never had a relationship with a dog like I had with Watachie. I was the center of his universe; he made me feel like I was someone worthwhile and incredibly special.

Watachie died too young, at the age of eight, leaving me with a gaping hole in my heart. But looking back, I know he accomplished what he set out to do. Not only was he a wonderful companion, but Watachie showed me my life's work. I found I enjoyed training dogs and loved teaching people how to train their own dogs. My article about Watachie and his early death was my first published article, and the responses to that article were my first "fan mail." I learned my writing could touch people. And, because of Watachie, I found out about purebred dog rescue. Because of Watachie, dogs became my calling, my joy and my profession.

Thanks, Watachie. I miss you still.

Love, Liz

• •

CHAPTER 1

TOO MANY DOGS AND NOT ENOUGH HOMES

In 2001, more than 55 percent of all American homes had at least one dog or cat, with a total of more than 60 million pet dogs in the United States, according to the Pet Food Institute. This group's report has been called the census of pet populations in the United States, and has tracked an increase in pet ownership over the past 20 years; in 1981, there were 54 million dogs in this country. This increase of six million dogs over two decades is somewhat deceiving, however, because it measures neither the number of dogs who have lost their homes, nor those who have been put to death because they had no homes.

RELINQUISHED DOGS

Although actual numbers vary from survey to survey, most experts agree that each year at least 25 percent of all dog-owning households will give up a dog. Dogs are given up for a variety of reasons; here are some of the more common ones:

- Moving, didn't want to take dog
- Moving to a place where dogs were not allowed
- Military owner transferred overseas
- Divorce
- No time for the dog
- Owner was ill or passed away
- Dog was found as a stray
- Family member brought home an unwanted dog

- Family member had allergies
- Couldn't afford the dog (including vet care)
- Didn't have a fenced yard
- Dog was an unwanted gift
- New baby in house; dog not trusted

As you can see, the dogs involved didn't cause any of these problems, yet they were the ones who lost their homes.

Unfortunately, not everyone is as committed to their dog as we would like them to be. But sadly, these are not the only reasons that dogs are given up. Many dogs are also given up due to what we call behavior problems. Here are the most common:

- Dog has bitten people
- Dog is aggressive to other dogs or other animals
- Neighbors complain of barking
- Dog is a destructive chewer
- Dog digs
- Dog jumps on people
- Owner is afraid of the dog

Again, the dogs are not to blame. All of these actions are natural behaviors for dogs. Granted, we may not like it when dogs bite, but it is their means of asserting themselves and the dogs do not understand why biting is a problem. It is our responsibility as dog owners to teach our dogs whether specific behaviors are acceptable, and if so, when. Obviously many people do not understand this, do not know how to control these behaviors or do not want to be bothered to teach their dog acceptable conduct.

Other reasons that dogs are given up are simply very, very sad:

- Owner bred their bitch, kept a puppy and got rid of the mother
- Dog didn't make it as a working dog and is no longer wanted
- Dog didn't make it as a show dog and is no longer wanted
- Stud dog is not breeding quality
- Owner is no longer showing or competing with the dog

Sometimes the owner just didn't understand dog ownership:

- Dog needed exercise
- Dog needed grooming
- Dog shed too much
- Dog needed training
- Dog had fleas

Regardless of the reason, millions of dogs are given up by their owners each year. Sometimes the circumstances are tragic; for example, when owners must give up their dogs because they need to move into a care facility where dogs are not allowed. Other times, dogs are given up because the owners were unprepared for the demands of dog ownership or because they chose a breed that wasn't right for them. Other times the reason seems frivolous. After all, most dog owners would agree that dogs need training, exercise and grooming.

WHEN DOGS ARE GIVEN UP

When giving up a dog, some owners act responsibly and work to find the dog a new home. Some spread the word among friends and co-workers, put an advertisement in the newspaper and screen new owners.

A great number of dogs given up by their owners are relinquished to shelters, pounds or humane societies. A decade ago, a dog given to a shelter would have probably been put to death within just a few days if

PUREBREDS AND MIXED BREEDS

Unfortunately, the supply of dogs exceeds the demand. There are not enough homes for all the puppies born. Although much of the blame for this excess has been laid at the feet of purebred dog breeders, they cannot assume all of the responsibility. Fully 50 percent of the puppies born are from accidental breedings, and most of them are mixed breed puppies. The other half are purebred puppies, of which only about 30 percent are or will be registered with the American Kennel Club or one of the other purebred dog registries.

he was not adopted. At that time, only 25 percent of dogs relinquished by their owners were adopted into new homes, but today the figure has increased dramatically. In many shelters, as many as 60 to 75 percent of all owner-relinquished dogs are adopted. That means, however, that 25 to 40 percent of the dogs are still being killed.

Some shelters (many self-described as "no kill") claim to have a 100 percent adoption rate. Although a 100 percent adoption rate is an awesome accomplishment, this figure can be deceptive. Some "no kill" shelters will not accept just any dog, and screen all dogs for temperament and health. Only those dogs who are adoptable (mentally and physically healthy with a reasonable chance of adjusting well in a new home) are accepted into their adoption program. While this is wonderful for those dogs accepted into the program, it leaves many dogs out who still need homes. Other shelters will accept all dogs, but their "no kill" rates do not include unadoptable dogs; only those considered adoptable. In other words, the fine print may (or should) read, "100 percent adoption rate for adoptable dogs."

Not all dogs given up by their owners are lucky enough to go to a new home or a shelter. Some dogs are turned loose to run as strays. A few lucky strays will be caught by animal control and brought to a shelter; the others will die of exposure, starvation, predators or will be casualties of collisions with vehicles.

CHANGING THESE STATISTICS

There is, obviously, no easy way to keep all dogs in their original home for their lifetime. As the adage says, "Stuff happens!" However, dogs do deserve a stable, caring home, and providing them with homes is undoubtedly the goal of all who love them.

Veterinary epidemiologist Philip Kass wanted to learn why so many dogs were given up by their owners and was a leader of the National Shelter Study. From April 1995 through April 1996, Kass and his co-investigators' goal was to uncover as much as possible about animals who are relinquished to shelters and the owners who bring them in. Kass found that the vast majority of people who gave up their pets were younger, less wealthy and less educated than the people who kept their pets. Many seemed to have little understanding of the requirements for successful pet ownership. They were uninformed of the importance of vaccinations, spaying, neutering and training.

Unfortunately, there are too many dogs and not enough homes for them.

Humane education of children in schools and communities has the potential to help change these statistics significantly. Children follow the lead of their parents, and if their parents are uneducated dog owners, then they will grow up with the same poor attitudes and expectations. However, if children learn what dogs are, how to care for them and why dogs act as they do, they are more likely to mature into responsible adult dog owners.

Adult education programs are a way of providing the same information to adults. Classes for potential and new dog owners may inform people about various dog breeds, dog behavior, obedience training, problem behavior and prevention, spaying and neutering and other aspects of dog care. Low-cost spay and neuter clinics and low-cost vaccination clinics have been proven to attract many people in communities across the country. Because clients often wait in line for services, educational programs being presented in the clinics could both entertain and educate pet owners while they wait.

Pet professionals need to work together, too, to promote responsible pet ownership. The pet community could sponsor seminars or have "dog days at the park" where professionals could share information. Veterinarians, animal control officials, dog club members, groomers and trainers could all participate.

Many shelters and humane societies today spay and neuter dogs prior to adoption, thereby removing those dogs from the future breeding pool. Breeders can do the same thing by having any non-show-quality puppies spayed or neutered before their sale. Admittedly, doing so would add to the breeders' costs, but the benefits to purebred dogs would be of great significance. Many purebred dog owners breed their dog because "there are champions in his pedigree" or because "I paid big money for this dog, I want to get my money back!" Poorly planned breedings obviously lead to more purebred dogs needing help in the future.

THE NEED FOR RESCUE

Until the number of dogs needing new homes declines dramatically, there will be a need for people to help find homes for dogs. There are, thankfully, many kindhearted, caring people who volunteer their time every week to help all dogs; mixed breeds and purebreds. And purebreds do need help, too. Although many people think only mixed breed dogs end up in shelters, that's not true. Take a walk through any shelter and you will see all types of purebred dogs side-by-side with mixed breeds.

About 20 years ago, the purebred dog rescue movement began when dog lovers realized that purebred dogs were facing the same problems as mixed breeds and dying at horrific rates in shelters. Concerned individuals, often breed club members, joined forces and formed groups to take in homeless dogs of their breed and find those dogs new homes. Thus, purebred dog rescue was born.

Purebred dog rescue is generally defined as the movement to find and care for purebred dogs in need, saving as many as possible from death, and placing those dogs in responsible, permanent homes. Rescue groups are working all over the world, and range in size from one-person operations that save one dog at a time to vast organizations run by, supported by or assisted by national breed clubs.

Because there is no governing agency for these groups, there are no concrete figures on how many dogs are saved each year. However, each group keeps its own records and the numbers can be staggering. For example, one Southern California Labrador Retriever rescue group saved and placed more than 350 Labs in one year alone. Multiply that number by all of the groups working across the country, and by all of the breeds needing help, and the totals could be astounding!

● ●

CHAPTER 2

PUREBRED DOG RESCUE

Recently, I took a walk through the local Humane Society and animal control shelter in Oceanside, California. My brief walk demonstrated the need for purebred dog rescue. Half of the dogs in the shelter on that day appeared to be purebred dogs. There were German Shepherd Dogs, Doberman Pinschers, Rottweilers, Golden Retrievers, Labrador Retrievers, Cocker Spaniels and Poodles. There was also a Papillon, a Yorkshire Terrier, a Border Terrier and a Dachshund. There were many obvious mixed breeds, too, but purebred dogs were abundant, and this great number of purebred dogs who need help is why rescue is so important.

SHELTER ADOPTIONS OR RESCUE ADOPTIONS?

Although both shelters and rescue programs share basically the same goal—to find homes for adoptable dogs—they do not provide precisely the same services. The most important difference between them is that the dog in a shelter may not have a known history. She may have been a stray, or she may have been given up by her owners with little information offered about her background. In addition, some state's privacy laws prevent public shelters from sharing information with prospective owners.

Rescue program volunteers, on the other hand, usually try to get as much information as possible about the dogs in their programs. When a dog is offered to a rescue program by her owner, the owner is asked quite a few questions or is asked to fill out a questionnaire. Some of the most commonly asked questions include:

- Is the dog housetrained?
- How often does she have an accident?
- Is the dog crate trained? Paper trained?

- Are the dog's shots up to date?
- Is the dog spayed or neutered?
- Do you have health records that you could share with the new owner?
- Does the dog have any health problems?
- Has the dog been to an obedience class?
- What skills, tricks and responses to commands does the dog know?
- What brand of dog food does the dog eat?
- How does the dog behave around people? Kids? Other dogs?
- Is the dog good with cats?
- What behavior problems does the dog have?
- What are the dog's favorite games? Toys?

With so much information available, potential owners can make an educated decision about whether this might be the right dog for them. They can decide if they have the time to housetrain an adult dog, or whether they are willing to train a dog who jumps on people. If they already have a cat or two in their home, they can make sure they choose a dog who is comfortable with cats.

Later, when the dog is adopted, knowing the dog's vocabulary and her favorite foods, games and toys can make the transition to a new home and family much easier.

Although most rescue groups prefer to take in dogs directly from their owners, some groups will accept dogs from shelters into their programs. These purebred dogs are thereby perhaps saved from death.

When dogs are accepted into the rescue programs from shelters with little or nothing known about their history, many rescue programs will have foster families take in the dogs. The dogs can then be evaluated as to temperament, habits and behaviors, and the dogs' obedience skills can be tested. By the time a possible adopter is found, many of the questions usually answered by an owner can be answered by the dog's foster family.

Rescue groups also screen the dogs they accept to avoid creating potentially dangerous situations. Aggressive dogs, or dogs who are known biters, are rarely (if ever) accepted into rescue programs. In comparison, the unknown history of some shelter dogs makes it difficult to screen for potentially dangerous dogs. For example, Aussie

FOSTER HOMES

Many rescue groups use networks of foster homes to care for homeless dogs until the right adoptive home is available. The foster home gives the dog a chance to settle down and live in a conventional home situation; unlike a kennel situation in a shelter. The foster family can assess the dog's behavior, help with training and get to know the dog. A foster owner can then provide information about that specific dog: "This is a very loving, affectionate dog who will do well with older kids although she seems leery of toddlers. She plays very well with other dogs but should not go to a home with cats, as she does chase them quite ferociously!" With firsthand information such as this, the rescue group has a better chance of making sure the dog is adopted into the right home.

Rescue & Placement Helpline (ARPH), a rescue organization for Australian Shepherds, has strict guidelines regarding behavior. No dog will be accepted into the program if she has a history of growling, snapping or biting. If, while the dog is in foster care, she shows aggressive behavior, she will be euthanized. Many other rescue groups, including the Bulldog Club of America Rescue program, have similar policies. While these policies may seem harsh, they're necessary. A dangerous dog cannot be adopted into a home situation where she could cause harm. Rescue volunteers must, first and foremost, adhere to moral, ethical and legal standards.

Some rescue groups also take in dogs considered unadoptable by many shelters. Yankee Golden Retriever Rescue (YGRR) has an excellent placement program for older Goldens, many of the dogs over eight years of age. YGRR will also accept Goldens with special medical needs and have helped dogs with epilepsy, vision problems, hearing loss and missing limbs find new homes. In most shelters, these dogs would have been considered unadoptable and would have been put to death.

BREED EXPERTS

Shelters deal with a variety of breeds and a host of mixed breeds. Most rescue groups focus on only one breed of dog and have volunteers who are very knowledgeable about their breed. Groups that assist with multiple breeds usually focus on similar breeds (such as setters or terriers) and maintain a list of experts for individual breeds. These experts are volunteers with experience and knowledge that they are willing to share.

Potential adopters can consult with these experts, ask questions and get real answers. Rescue volunteers rarely try to "sell" their breed or talk people into adopting a dog from their program. After all, a major reason the group exists is that people choose the wrong breed. Instead, rescue volunteers are more concerned with making sure the right people choose their breed, and they will usually give honest, forthright answers to questions about the breed. Each breed has its own unique characteristics, and potential owners need to know what these are so they can decide if this is the right type of dog for their family, home and lifestyle.

Some rescue groups ask that owners giving up their dog first speak with a knowledgeable volunteer. After learning more about their breed or getting some help, some owners decide to keep their dog. Cynthia Knowles of Manassas, Virginia, had gotten a Rottweiler puppy because her husband was serving in the Marine Corps and was often away from home. "I wanted a dog to keep me company but also to keep me safe. I worry about living alone sometimes," she explained. When her Rottie puppy didn't show any signs of protectiveness, she thought that perhaps her puppy didn't have the temperament she desired. When, at eight months of age, he still wasn't being protective, Knowles was ready to give up on him. "He loves everyone! I was sure that if a burglar tried to come in, he would welcome him with kisses!" However, a Rottweiler rescue volunteer explained to Knowles that Rotties are very slow to mature, and as adults they do develop a wonderfully protective nature. The volunteer also explained to Knowles that her puppy sounded like he had a nice temperament and was perfectly normal for a puppy his age. After the discussion with the Rottweiler expert, Knowles decided to keep her dog and give him time to grow up.

A Sampling of Purebred Rescue Groups

There are hundreds of rescue groups all over the country. Some are managed by a handful of people and rescue one dog at a time; others have many volunteers and take in many dogs. Some of the groups foster all of the dogs they rescue; others serve primarily as referral agencies and match up people who want to give up a dog with people looking to adopt one. Although each of these groups is unique, one thing they all have in common is a desire to save dogs.

*Many rescue groups ask relinquishing owners to talk to
a breed expert before they give up their dog.*

It would be impossible to describe here all of the groups doing this good work. However, I do want to highlight a few groups to portray how they work. Each has a similar goal, but the group's approach to that goal will be its own.

SEATTLE PUREBRED DOG RESCUE

Seattle Purebred Dog Rescue (SPDR, www.spdrdogs.org) was founded in 1987 and is an all-volunteer, not-for-profit organization dedicated to placing purebred dogs into carefully screened homes in the Puget Sound area of Washington State. The goal of SPDR is to offer dog owners an alternative to taking an unwanted purebred to the shelter.

Working as an adoption referral service by networking with the local dog fancy, the group can find dogs new homes and, as a result, local shelters can lower their rate of dogs who are put to death.

SPDR maintains a list of breed experts who screen the dogs offered to the group. These experts can spot potential behavior problems that might eliminate the dog from the program (such as aggressive behavior toward people). The experts can also provide breed-specific advice to owners who are thinking of giving up their dog, and to those considering adopting a dog of that particular breed.

In its first few years of operation, SPDR placed between 200 and 300 dogs annually. In 1995, more than 3,000 dogs came into SPDR's program, and in recent years, the group has handled more than 3,500 dogs annually.

YANKEE GOLDEN RETRIEVER RESCUE, INC.

Yankee Golden Retriever Rescue (YGRR, www.ygrr.org) was established in 1985 by Joan Puglia and Susan Foster when both women noticed an increase in the number of Goldens found in local shelters. Based in Massachusetts, YGRR serves the New England states.

Along with saving hundreds of healthy young Goldens, YGRR has served as a model for other rescue groups for its work with older dogs and those with special needs, including Goldens who need ongoing veterinary care. YGRR placed its 2,000th Golden in 1996 and in 2000 placed Golden number 3,000—a notable achievement!

AUSSIE RESCUE & PLACEMENT HELPLINE

The Aussie Rescue & Placement Helpline (ARPH, www.aussie rescue.org) is dedicated to saving Australian Shepherds. With volunteers all over the country, ARPH works as a referral system, bringing together people wanting to give up a dog and those wishing to adopt one. The group also has an extensive network of foster homes, so that dogs needing a place to stay right away do not have to go to or remain in a shelter or kennel.

ARPH also provides information on the unique temperament, intelligence, exercise needs and training requirements of the breed.

"SORTA" BEARDIES

Bearded Collie rescue volunteers have found a way to help those dogs who appear to be "almost" Bearded Collies. A freestanding organization (not under the parent club umbrella) called BONE (Beardies or Neardies) was formed to rescue and place these dogs. The group has been quite successful.

NATIONAL BREED CLUBS

The American Kennel Club (AKC, www.akc.org) recognizes a national breed club for each of the breeds it registers. This parent club governs or supervises many of the activities within the breed, and this usually includes rescue efforts. Some clubs have rescue efforts organized at the national club level, while others delegate the work to regional or local clubs. Other clubs prefer to keep rescue efforts separate from club activities and have an independent organization for rescue. In most cases, the parent club provides financial help to the rescue group.

The AKC's monthly magazine, the *AKC Gazette*, maintains a list of club rescue programs that is published every November. For the most recent list, go to AKC's web site.

RESCUE EFFORTS TODAY AND TOMORROW

When discussing the future, most rescue group volunteers mention two things: a lack of money and the never-ending supply of dogs who need help.

Bonnie Guzman, co-founder of the Fox Terrier Network, said, "The biggest issue for Fox Terrier rescue is, in my opinion, money. There is never enough. Rescue is grinding, emotionally exhausting work, but all of this is compounded when money is short." She continued, "Many dogs coming into rescue have medical issues that need to be taken care of prior to making the dog available for adoption."

Guzman said the Fox Terrier rescue volunteers have tried most of the standard means of fund-raising, including rescue fairs, newsletters and bake sales. They also request donations when dogs are adopted. Guzman said, "We have many loyal Fox Terrier owners who, if we are destitute, we can call and ask for help, and often they will help. We are very fortunate for supporters like these."

Some clubs receive some financial assistance from their parent club, but this assistance rarely covers all of the group's costs. In most cases, rescue groups must spend time and energy raising funds as well as rescuing and placing dogs.

The unending numbers of dogs needing help weighs down many rescue volunteers and groups, too. Kim Galloway, the AKC National Rescue Coordinator for American Eskimo Dogs, said, "The biggest problem I have today is the sheer number of dogs needing homes and not nearly enough potential homes for them. There are not nearly enough foster homes, either. I know I can't save them all, but I have to give each and every one a chance."

Although many of the dogs needing rescue come from breeders, some also come from pet owners who have bred their dog. American Eskimo Dogs (as with so many other breeds) have also attracted the attention of puppy mill breeders. Galloway said, "My breed is a relatively healthy breed, but because they are such beautiful dogs and incredibly cute puppies, they are exploited by the puppy mills. This is a breed that must be socialized at an early age to avoid problems in the future. Lack of socialization and poor breeding often lead to aggression and biting problems, and these problems are what cause the dogs to be turned over to rescue."

No one involved with rescue sees rescue work diminishing at any time in the foreseeable future. In fact, more and more shelters are working with purebred rescue groups. As shelters strive to place all of the adoptable dogs taken in, the more dogs the rescue groups can place, the better!

• •

CHAPTER 3

IS A RESCUE DOG
RIGHT FOR YOU?

The decision to add a dog to your life is not one to be made lightly or on impulse. You must first evaluate your needs and the needs of your family. You should think carefully about why you want a dog. Ask yourself: What do I want in a dog? Are the breeds I'm considering able to fulfill my desires? Purchasing or adopting a dog is a long-term commitment; with good care most dogs will live 12 to 14 years. Before you make any decision, make sure you know how a dog will affect your life.

In addition, you must understand that most rescue dogs, even young ones, come with some baggage. If the dog was well loved and cared for, and lost his owners through circumstances beyond his control, he may be grieving for them. Another dog may have been neglected, emotionally and physically, and may need extensive rehabilitation. Some dogs have had no training and little socialization, and others have been spoiled rotten. A baby puppy from a reputable breeder is a clean slate, but a rescue dog is not. He will usually have one or more needs that require rehabilitation of some kind. Make sure you know what you're getting into and are ready for the challenges a rescue dog may provide.

QUESTIONS TO ASK YOURSELF

Read the following pages carefully and be honest with yourself. No one is judging your answers—the goal is to steer you down the right path to happy dog ownership.

YOUR MONEY

Can you afford a dog? Although it may seem coldhearted to think about costs before anything else, dogs can be expensive. You may need to do some shopping prior to bringing home a dog and those supplies (including a high-quality dog food) will cost money. The rescue group will request a donation when you adopt the dog. The amount will vary, but the request is usually for $100 to $200 (or more if the dog needed veterinary care). Regular veterinary care is an ongoing expense. As a general rule, plan on spending between $3,000 and $5,000 for the first year of dog ownership. If the dog is healthy, expenses during the following years should be lower, but make sure you have the financial reserves for emergencies.

YOUR LIFESTYLE

Do you have the time for a dog? Dogs require a substantial time commitment from you. Very few dogs are happy to be alone in the backyard for hours at a time; most prefer to be with their people. Dogs left alone for long periods will begin to bark and dig up the garden. Some will even harm themselves by chewing on a part of their body. Plan on taking the time to walk the dog, play with the dog and groom the dog. And plan on just hanging out with him.

Why do you want a dog? Do you want companionship? Do you want a jogging partner? Do you want a dog for personal protection? Make an honest wish list and examine it carefully. This will help you choose the right dog. If you want a jogging partner, don't get a Rottweiler; they are powerful but are not long-distance runners. If you want a personal protection dog, don't get a Golden Retriever; that's not their job!

Do you like to exercise? All dogs need exercise, although some breeds need more than others. If you dislike long walks, hate bicycle riding and don't jog, consider a breed that has minimal exercise requirements. If you like to run, love riding a bike, love to throw the Frisbee and enjoy time outside, then get a dog with higher exercise needs.

Can you groom a dog? Every dog needs regular grooming, but the fluffy and longhaired breeds need more than the shorthaired ones. And don't expect shorthaired dogs not to shed; they do! They just shed short hairs instead of long ones. All dogs of all coat types need their ears and teeth cleaned and toenails trimmed. When you are making a decision

Do you have time for a dog? Dogs require a substantial time commitment.

about a particular breed, take its grooming needs into consideration. Make sure you can, and are willing to, provide what the dog needs to be well groomed.

Are you willing to train the dog? Training requires time, consistency and patience from you. Although all dogs need training, some breeds are more receptive to training than others. Keep in mind that the dog who dislikes training, the one who will defy or challenge you, is also the one who needs training the most!

Does everyone in the household want a new dog? If you want a new dog but others in the home do not, you may want to rethink your decision. Even one person could make life difficult for the dog. One person's animosity, lack of caring, anger, neglect or even abuse could severely traumatize or harm the dog. Everyone should be in agreement regarding the dog.

Do you have even more time? Small chores require time, too. The dog's feces need to be picked up in the backyard. The dog's water needs to be changed daily and of course, the dog needs to be fed daily. Time should be allocated for exercise and play, for cuddling, training and grooming. A dog will take up more time than you will expect.

TAKE MAX WITH YOU WHEN YOU MOVE!

My husband spent twenty years in the U.S. Marine Corps and this required us to pack up and move on a regular basis. As dogs are an important part of our lives, this meant moving the dogs, too, as well as other pets. Although many people use moving as an excuse to get rid of a dog, moving with a dog isn't that hard. To a dog, moving is a grand adventure! As long as you are there, he doesn't care where he lives. One of our most exiting moves was from Virginia to Southern California with a German Shepherd, a Doberman, a cat, a cockatoo, and a Burmese python. But we all made it and were soon settled into a new house that quickly became our home. All it takes is some prior planning and a lot of patience.

YOUR HOME AND POSSESSIONS

Will a dog fit into your living arrangements? Dogs take up physical space and if you live in a tiny studio apartment, a Saint Bernard might cover your entire floor. Apartment dwellers should also avoid those breeds known to be barkers. Also, if you live in an apartment, a condo, or a rented house, do you need permission from your landlord to get a dog?

How much do you value your possessions? If you like an immaculate, pristine house, perhaps you should consider a ceramic dog rather than a live one. Dogs can be messy. Dogs track in dirt, shed (some shed a lot!) and can knock things over. Dogs, especially young ones, can be destructive chewers. Dogs' tails have been known to clean off the coffee table in one sweep. It's amazing how powerful a tail can be!

Is your yard securely fenced? Some breeds are known to be escape artists, especially if left alone too long. Some newly adopted dogs suffer from separation anxiety and will panic if left outside by themselves. Is your yard big enough for a Greyhound to run around in or is it better suited to a Pomeranian? Would it bother you if the dog tried to dig up a gopher? Some breeds are more prone to digging than others.

Where do you see yourself in five years? Are you climbing the corporate ladder and facing possible transfers? Will you be retiring soon and moving? Are you willing to take the dog's future with you into consideration? A dog is a 12- to 14-year (or more!) commitment. If there is any doubt as to whether you will be able to keep the dog for his lifetime, think about that now. Of course, you can't see the future and all that it may entail, but if you're not sure of your commitment, don't adopt a dog.

THE BREED (OR BREEDS) FOR YOU

Do you have memories of a Shetland Sheepdog who washed away your tears as a child? Were you impressed by the dedication and skill of a German Shepherd Dog guiding his blind master? You can take those personal preferences into consideration when choosing a dog, but don't set any type of dog on a pedestal. Keep in mind that your childhood memories probably have an element of fantasy. You may remember that Sheltie's tender qualities but you may not remember how many times your mother told the dog to stop barking. And that German Shepherd guide dog had a *lot* of training.

Every breed of dog was "designed" or bred for a specific purpose. That purpose can greatly affect the dog as a pet and companion. Herding dogs, for example, are active, athletic animals who will want to herd you, the kids and the family cats. Scenthounds are happiest when

Every breed was developed for a purpose. Bloodhounds are the ultimate scenting dogs.

EVALUATE YOURSELF

This quick evaluation should help you organize your thoughts as you think about your future best friend. Answer the questions candidly, as you are today; not as you would like yourself to be tomorrow!

1. When you come home from work you are:
   A. Tired and just want to relax; you spend the evening reading or watching television.
   B. Tired but like to get outside, walking or riding your bicycle.
   C. Glad to get home, can't wait to do something.

   If you answered A, you should consider a calm, older dog or a stuffed animal. If you answered B, a calm, younger dog might suit you. If you answered C, an active, young dog should please you.

2. Being the center of a dog's world can be thrilling to some people and overwhelming to others. Do you:
   A. Like being the center of someone's attention?
   B. Like the idea of a dog who follows your every move?
   C. Prefer a dog who is more independent?
   D. Dislike being followed or watched? Do you dislike being touched?

their nose is vacuuming odors from the ground. These dogs will, when off leash, follow their nose anywhere, and without training (and sometimes even with training) will ignore your commands or pleas to "come!" Sighthounds love to run and run very, very fast. This habit can get them into trouble, running in front of cars or chasing down the family cat. So, think of your personal preferences as to breed, and then think of what that breed was designed to do. Will the dog's innate working qualities fit into your family life today?

While mulling over your personal preference as to a breed, keep an open mind. There are more than 400 dog breeds worldwide. The differences between some breeds and others are immense (think of Great Danes and Chihuahuas!) but with other breeds the distinctions are more subtle. Australian Shepherds and English Shepherds, for example,

If you answered yes to A or B, many types of dog will suit your needs. You are a particularly good candidate for a dog of the working or herding breeds. If you answered C, think about some of the hounds or terriers. If you answered D, get a ceramic dog.

3. What is your lifestyle?

   A. Are you retired and live alone?

   B. Do you work and live alone or with one other adult?

   C. Are there active children in the household?

   D. Do you have some health problems that might affect your life with a dog?

If you answered yes to A, you might want a dog who is entertaining and somewhat active. However, if both A and D describe you, you will want a dog who is entertaining but less rambunctious. If you answered yes to B, you may need a breed or personality that can stay home alone while you're both at work, or you may want to get a cat instead. If you answered yes to C, you should look for a medium- to large-sized dog with a calm personality who can handle the stimulation of the kids.

share many characteristics. Aussies are recognized by the AKC and have either a natural bobtail or a docked tail; English Shepherds (ES's to their friends) are not recognized by the AKC and have a long, full tail. However, the two breeds share similar activity levels, a desire to work and easy trainability. Some breeds, moreover, have very long waiting lists for adoption. If you are willing to consider other breeds, you may find that special dog sooner rather than later.

Keep in mind, too, that although most dogs of a particular breed have common characteristics, each dog is also an individual. Some Shelties are horrible barkers (even Sheltie breeders will admit that!), while others are quieter and less reactive. Some German Shepherds are easily trained and are dedicated to their work, while others are much more difficult to train. Each dog is an individual.

A QUICK LOOK AT BREED TRAITS

- Sporting dogs are active, very aware of small animals and birds, and need lots of exercise. Most are quite trainable although a few breeds can be somewhat stubborn.
- Scenthounds are independent hunters and as such, independent thinkers. They love to use their nose! Scent hounds are bright but not as easy to train as many other breeds.
- Sighthounds are very visually oriented and notice every movement. Although couch potatoes when resting, they love to run! Sighthounds can be trained when the owner finds the right motivation.
- Working dogs love to work and need a job. Most are easily trained and most need daily, vigorous exercise. Many are quite protective.
- Toy dogs were bred as companions. Most are receptive to training and thrive on it.
- Terriers are a challenge! They are quick, intelligent, funny and feisty. Terriers can be wonderful companions for people who share their characteristics.
- Herding dogs are active, athletic dogs. They are focused, intelligent and need a job to do. They are easily trained but also easily bored.
- Livestock guarding dogs are protective, sometimes to a fault, and bark loudly when alarmed. They respond best to training when they understand the need for it.
- Non-sporting dogs vary in size, temperament and many other characteristics. Each non-sporting breed must really be considered separately.

WHY ADOPT A RESCUE DOG?

The vast majority of dogs coming into rescue programs are adults. They may be as young as one or two years old or they may be quite elderly. Most rescue groups say the average is three years of age. Very few rescue groups see many puppies, especially very young ones. Because most dogs available for adoption are adults, those adopting the dogs don't have to cope with the normal puppy problems. Many potential adopters would prefer to skip the crying, whining, chewing and housetraining that come with a very young puppy.

Other potential adopters simply prefer adult dogs. Not everyone finds puppies cute or attractive. Harlan Jacobson of Hartford, Connecticut, said, "I guess I just don't have the nurturing instinct or whatever it's called. Puppies are too helpless, too demanding and take too long to grow up. I like dogs; grown-up dogs." Other people don't feel they have the patience to raise a puppy. Tom Baker of San Diego, California, is an active man and likes adult dogs, "I jog, ride a bike, and hike. I'd like to share my outings with a dog but I don't have the patience to wait for a puppy to grow up." For people who prefer adult dogs, rescue dogs can be perfect.

Although there are other practical reasons people adopt an adult dog rather than buy a puppy, the most common reason is that people enjoy saving a dog's life. Jonathon Baker adopted a Siberian Husky from a south Texas rescue group. Baker explained, "I had wanted a dog for a while and did a lot of research as to the breeds I was interested in. I finally decided on a Siberian Husky. I talked to some breeders and got on a waiting list for a couple of future litters. Then one day I went to a dog show and walked over to watch the obedience competition. I saw a woman and her black and silver Siberian work in one of the advanced classes. I was astounded."

He continued, "Since I had done a lot of research on this breed, I knew that the kind of obedience skills required for the advanced classes were not really among the breed's strong points. So I waited until they were done and went over to talk. That's when I found out about Siberian Husky rescue. The dog had been picked up by rescue from a neglectful and possibly abusive owner." Baker called a local Siberian Husky rescue group and learned they had several adult dogs ready to be adopted. He met Racer, took him home and they have been companions for three years now. Baker added, "Racer might have been euthanized had the rescue group not stepped in, and had I not adopted him. It's a good feeling."

RESCUE REPERCUSSIONS

Joann Schmitz of Las Vegas owns only rescue dogs. She wouldn't think of buying a dog from a breeder, "I like the idea that these dogs needed me; that my actions saved their life." Schmitz continued, "I work full-time, care for my family and do some volunteer work. I'm always busy.

But it was still hard to see where my efforts made any difference in the world. But when I adopted these dogs, I knew I made a difference in their lives."

Schmitz's desire to save a dog's life is not unusual. We have all seen the flyers and advertisements showing a sad-faced dog with huge eyes under a banner, "I need a home!" People who adopt a dog in need feel good about it. There's a sense of satisfaction in knowing that a life was saved.

Rescuing a dog can also give people a sense of contribution toward the world we live in. My neighbor rescued a Pit Bull who was confiscated from a man who bred dogs for dogfighting. She said, "I feel powerless to stop wars; make a difference to homeless people or solve the drug problem. But I can save a creature who would have otherwise been euthanized." Her decision has not been an easy one, though. She said, "Rocky is too aggressive to walk out in public; he does want to fight other dogs. But he's a great dog at home."

While the decision to rescue a dog may take some thought, it is over relatively quickly. Living with that decision can be much more difficult. The dog my neighbor adopted is young and will live up to 12 more years. So she will live with a big, powerful, dog-aggressive dog for many years to come. She will not be able to have another dog, a cat or even a rabbit because her adopted dog has shown the desire to attack other living creatures.

My neighbor's situation may seem extreme but it really isn't. Many other adopters have been placed in similar situations. Cathy Cousins of Vista, California, adopted a young, deaf Dalmatian from a Dalmatian rescue group. There is a lot of help for the owners of deaf dogs and Cousins has enrolled in a training class with a dog trainer who has worked with deaf dogs. But until Cousins brought home her new dog, named Silence, she had no idea what was involved with a disabled dog, "I thought I could just use hand signals and communicate with Silence. I didn't think about all the other aspects of living with a deaf animal. When she raids the trash can, I can't just yell at her and tell her to stop it. When she dashes out the front door, I can't call her to come. When she's sleeping I have to make sure the kids don't startle her awake. It really has been a difficult transition."

People considering adopting rescue dogs—especially dogs with disabilities, injuries, illnesses, behavior problems or troubled pasts—need to carefully think about the future prior to adopting that dog. Although a kind, loving home can mend many problems, it cannot solve them all. The truth is that too many adopted dogs end up back in rescue. People fall in love with a dog, take the dog home and then get hit with a severe case of reality. The problems that didn't seem so big before are tremendous when faced on a daily basis. Eventually the dog is returned to the rescue group.

And so the decision to adopt a dog should be one part emotion, and many parts realism. Keep feelings in check long enough to choose the right dog for you and your family. And then adopt the dog with the belief that you can—you will—make this work!

• •

CHAPTER 4

THE ADOPTION PROCESS

After quite a bit of research, Kathy Simons of Fairbanks, Alaska, decided that she wanted an Australian Shepherd. Simons was very active, worked part-time at home, and liked to do things outside, even in the winter. She knew she could keep an Aussie busy and she liked training. But Simons also wanted to avoid the hassles of puppyhood and decided that a young adult dog from rescue would suit her well, "I knew that a dog from rescue might have some problems, but I have also heard that Aussies are flexible and as a rule, they settle quickly into new homes." Although Simons was ready for a dog right away, she found out that making the decision was the easy (and quick) part of the process; finally bringing home a dog often comes much later.

FINDING A RESCUE GROUP

The first thing you need to do, obviously, is find a rescue group for the breed (or breeds) you're looking for. Local humane societies and shelters usually maintain a list of rescue groups in the area. Some rescue groups also have long-running advertisements in the local newspapers, often in the "Dogs for Sale" section of the classified ads. You may also want to call several local veterinarians and ask if they know of a rescue group for your desired breed.

Sometimes, dog-related publications such as *AKC Gazette, Dog Fancy* and *DogWorld* carry ads for rescue groups. The *AKC Gazette* publishes a list of rescue groups for the national breed clubs in each November issue. The national representatives or coordinators can point you toward a regional or local club. For more information, go to www.akc.org.

The Internet has been a wonderful tool for rescue efforts. Most rescue work is done through networking; people talk to other people about dogs who are available, about dogs needing foster homes, and about people looking for a dog. The Internet is the ultimate networking tool, and rescuers have taken advantage of it.

If you search the word for your potential breed plus the word "rescue" plus your local region, you could find one or more rescue groups. For example, I went to Google (www.google.com) and in the search box typed "Australian Shepherd + rescue + San Diego" and the search turned up several very promising sites. Some of the sites had links to everything Aussie, including rescue groups, and several were web sites specifically for Aussie rescue efforts.

EVALUATING THE RESCUE GROUP

Rescue groups vary from one-person operations to large national organizations supported in whole or in part by national breed clubs. As a rule, neither is better or worse than the other. You will, however, want to make sure the rescue group is legitimate, will assist you in your adoption efforts and will be there for you later should you need help.

Every group, regardless of its size, should have some written guidelines, and often the group's web site will have the guidelines posted. These should state how the organization is run, whether it's a not-for-profit organization and what its policies are concerning how dogs are accepted into the program and how the adoption process works. Examine these guidelines closely, and make sure you are comfortable with them, particularly the fee structure and the provisions about

BE AN EDUCATED CONSUMER

Unfortunately, there are some less-than-scrupulous individuals involved in breed rescue activities. Some charge unconscionably high fees to accept a dog into a rescue program and some charge outrageous fees for adopting a dog. Some will place a dog with known behavior or health problems with unsuspecting new owners. Some try to use guilt to get people to adopt an unsuitable dog. Adopting a rescue dog is often an emotional decision and endeavor. However, to protect yourself, be an educated consumer. Read the fine print, ask questions and ask for several references before making any decision.

adopting the dog to a new home. If problems arise, you want to know how the organization will address them. Take a look, too, at the adoption application and contract. Be certain that you understand these documents and do not object to any of the questions or terms, prior to filling them out.

Once you've read the guidelines, talk to a rescue group volunteer. Ask for clarification of the guidelines if necessary. Ask about their adoption contract and how the adoption process works. Ask, too, about the breed. Most rescue volunteers are more than happy to answer your questions about their breed and about the rescue group they are working with. No question is stupid. However, if you feel uncomfortable with a particular volunteer, or with the group itself, go somewhere else. In this situation, don't hesitate to move on.

Remember that rescue volunteers are just that—volunteers. Most do this work from their homes. When you call, they may have voice mail answer, or they may ask you to call back at another time. If they do, don't get angry. They may be eating dinner, putting the kids to bed or feeding their own dogs.

THE APPLICATION AND INSPECTION

Once you are comfortable with the rescue group, fill out an adoption application. Most groups today request that you do so prior to being shown any dogs. Applications will generally ask the following:

> Name
>
> Address
>
> Phone
>
> E-mail
>
> Occupation and length of employment
>
> Personal references (two)
>
> Do you own or rent your home?
>
> If you rent, do you have your landlord's permission to have a dog? Landlord's name and phone number?
>
> How long have you lived at your current address?
>
> Is your yard fenced? What kind of fence do you have? How tall is it?

Do you have a dog run? What is the height and size of the run?

Where will the dog spend her time during the day? At night?

On average, how many hours every day will the dog be alone?

How many adults live in the household?

How many children live in the home? What are their ages and genders?

Do you own any other dogs? What are their ages, sexes and breeds?

What has happened to any dogs you have owned previously but no longer own?

Do you have any other pets? What kind?

Who is your veterinarian? Name and phone number?

Why are you applying for a _____ (breed) rescue dog?

Why do you want this dog? Do you want a dog for a pet, for competition, for hunting, or for some other purpose?

Once you have completed the application, submit it according to directions. Some groups ask that you mail it in, while others accept only e-mail applications. Most groups ask that you wait a week or two prior to inquiring about your application's status. It takes time to contact your references and almost all groups *do* verify those references. Also, many groups receive quite a few applications and processing them simply takes time.

When your application has been accepted, the representative from the rescue group will want to make an appointment to inspect your house and yard. They will want to verify that you live where you say you do, and that the yard is securely fenced. In addition, group members may have a few more questions for you.

Don't take offense at the questions in the application, the inspection or any follow-up investigation. The group is not trying to invade your privacy or "grill" you. Instead, they're trying to find the very best homes possible for dogs who have already been through the trauma of losing a home. By being very careful, group members hope to put their dogs into homes where the dogs can stay for the rest of their lives. So be patient and allow the process to happen.

If your application is turned down, please listen to the rescue volunteer's explanation. Mary Ellen Berger, a Rescue Rep for the Italian Greyhound Club of America and the Italian Greyhound Safehouse

WHY SO CAUTIOUS?

Seasoned rescue volunteers are very careful when evaluating a potential adopter. Remarkably enough, some potential adopters lie about where they live, whether their yard is fenced, and about who lives in the house. One of the most common misrepresentations concerns owning or renting a home. Many renters say they own the house, then bring the dog back to rescue later because their landlord won't allow the dog. Other people represent themselves as potential adopters when they are really buying dogs for resale, often to research labs. So be patient with the rescue volunteer; those questions and inspections have a purpose.

Alliance, said, "Turning down adopters is something nobody enjoys. We don't do it because we hate the applicant, or because we're snobby, or because the applicant isn't rich enough. We do it so we can sleep at night. Our foster dogs have many times been through a lot before they get into rescue, and we want nothing more than to provide each and every one of them a permanent, loving, safe new home." She continued, "I will honestly tell someone why he was denied. Maybe it's something that the person can change and maybe it's a real philosophical difference. It's still my decision and I have to live with the consequences of a potential failure." Unfortunately some people take denials hard. Berger says some rescue volunteers have even been threatened!

MEETING DOGS

Once your application has been approved, you have met with a rescue volunteer and your house and yard have been inspected, then it's time to start looking at dogs. Some rescue groups have descriptions of dogs posted on their web site, complete with photos. This is an easy way to see many dogs quickly but it doesn't really tell you much about the dog's personality and temperament. That requires seeing and meeting the dogs.

Before you go look at numerous dogs, tell the rescue volunteer exactly what you're looking for in a dog. For example, I like outgoing dogs who are not too dominant. I like dogs who like to play, especially retrieving games with balls and Frisbees. I prefer males and my males are always neutered. I do not want or need a show quality dog, as I don't compete in conformation; however, I do many other things with my dogs including carting, agility, obedience and therapy dog work. And I'm partial to black tri-colored dogs. By giving the rescue volunteers my preferences, I can help them try to narrow down the search for me. They can make a list of male, tri-colored dogs who are extroverts and who like to play! They can weed out the dogs who would not suit my personal needs.

DON'T BE BASHFUL

When the rescue volunteer calls and says there is a dog available for you to meet, ask questions! This is not the time to be shy. Sarah Filipiak, president of Pound Rescue of Athens, Ohio, said, "When contacting a

*Tell the rescue volunteer what you want from a dog
and what you want to do with your new dog.*

rescue about a specific dog, be prepared with a list of questions. Often I will begin by asking, 'What can I tell you about Bella?' only to be met with the reply, 'I don't know.'" Filipiak continued, "Some good questions could include: Does she get along with cats? Where does she sleep in her foster home? Is she crate trained? Is she good with kids? What games does she like to play?" Filipiak also said, "Thoughtful questions from potential adopters tell me they are serious about giving the dog a good home, and they didn't just see a photo and make an impulsive decision."

Some questions you might want to ask the rescue volunteer prior to meeting the dog include:

> How did the dog lose her first home?
>
> Where is the dog now? Is she in a foster home or a kennel?
>
> How long has the dog been there? How is she reacting to the changes?
>
> How does she react to men? Women? Children?
>
> Is she good with other dogs? Cats? Other animals?
>
> How old is she? Has she been spayed (or if appropriate, neutered)?
>
> How is her health?
>
> Does she need any veterinary care right now?
>
> Does she have any known health problems?
>
> What is her personality like?
>
> Does she like to play?
>
> When playing, does she get overly exuberant?
>
> Does she stop playing when the game is over?
>
> Has she had any training? How much?
>
> Does she follow standard obedience commands?
>
> How are her household manners? Does she get up on the furniture or raid the trash can?
>
> Does she have any known bad habits or behavior problems?

Once you have the answers to as many of these questions as possible, then you can decide whether to meet this dog. If the dog has some problems you would prefer not to manage, then do not arrange to meet

> ## USE YOUR BRAIN AND *THEN* YOUR HEART
>
> When you go to meet a dog, go with the knowledge that you will not accept the first dog you see. Even if you fall in love with her, go see two or three others just to make sure you're making the right decision. So gird those proverbial loins before you go!

her. Don't waste the time of the volunteer and put yourself through that emotional trauma. And don't let the rescue volunteer make you feel guilty, either! You're the one who would have the long-term commitment to the dog, and will have to live with the dog, so make the best decision you can for yourself and your family. Guilt has no place in that decision.

YOUR INITIAL ASSESSMENT

When you first meet the dog, observe her for a few minutes before greeting her. Watch how she interacts with the foster owners and rescue volunteers. She is probably comfortable with them, especially her foster owners, and her conduct with them will give you a genuine picture of her personality. Ask them to interact with her: groom her, play ball with her and cuddle her. If after watching her for a while, you think she looks like a dog you would like to get to know better, ask to interact with her. Don't force yourself on her, but encourage her to approach you. Sit on a low stool (but not the floor), encourage her to come close for some petting. Ask the foster owners if you can offer her a treat. Throw the ball for her and ask her to bring it back to you.

Once you have spent some time with her, ask if you can take her for a walk. Watch her behavior outside. Practice some obedience training—very gently, of course, with lots of praise.

FOLLOW-UP

Now is also the time to ask more questions. Ask her foster parents anything that concerns you. Why is she favoring her right rear leg? Does she seem worried about the vacuum cleaner? When walking her, you noticed she pulls hard on the leash; has she had any obedience training? This is the time to voice any concerns and get answers.

Don't adopt the first dog you meet,
even if you fall in love with that wonderful face.

By now you should be getting a feeling about the dog, but as I said earlier, don't make a commitment right away. Let the rescue volunteers know whether you are interested in her. If you are, be clear that you would still like to see one or two more dogs just to make sure you're making the right decision.

Don't let anyone make you feel guilty about not making an immediate decision. Sometimes rescue volunteers will be so focused on placing a dog, they will put pressure on the potential adopter: "If you don't take her right now, someone else will adopt her! I have three people coming this afternoon!" Don't permit yourself to be influenced by a volunteer's eagerness or a volunteer's pressure. You are making a decision you will have to live with for 12 to 14 years. Make the best decision you can.

WHEN YOU'VE FOUND THE RIGHT DOG

After seeing a few more dogs, you're ready to select one. You may decide that the first dog was perfect for you after all, or maybe the third dog struck just the right chord.

Once you have found the dog for you, notify the rescue volunteers. They will ask you to sign an adoption contract. Sometimes this is a part of the adoption application you already completed and sometimes it is a separate document altogether. One of the primary reasons that you are asked to sign a contract is symbolic: the volunteers want to make sure that you and other future dog owners understand that this dog is important, both to them and to you.

Most adoption contracts include your personal information: name, address, telephone number and the like. Then the dog is identified: breed, coloring, markings, sex and any other identification including tattoo or microchip. There is usually a liability release and the terms of the adoption. Most groups require that the dog be returned to the group should the adoption prove unsatisfactory. There is usually a section detailing owner responsibilities, which may state required veterinary care, grooming, and so forth.

Seattle Purebred Dog Rescue has a Terms of Adoption contract that all adopters must sign. It contains the following terms:

If I am successful in the adoption of a dog through SPDR I agree to the following conditions:

1. To keep this dog in my personal possession, and to provide proper and sufficient food, water, shelter, grooming and humane treatment at all times.

2. To spay or neuter this dog within 30 days of adoption at my expense if the dog is not already altered. Proof of spaying or neutering will be provided in writing to SPDR within ten days of surgery. I will not allow this dog to breed under any circumstances.

3. To procure veterinary care at once if this dog is sick or injured, and to keep current all vaccinations as recommended by my dog's veterinarian.

4. To provide this dog with an identification tag secured to a buckle collar which will be worn at all times. In addition, SPDR

recommends tattooing and/or microchipping as a means of permanent identification.

5. To obey any and all animal control regulations governing the area in which I live, and to license this dog according to such regulations within one month of adoption.

6. Not to sell, trade, transfer ownership, abandon, or dispose of this dog in any way, but to notify SPDR if I must relinquish custody of the dog. This includes release to family members.

7. To allow an SPDR representative to examine the dog and its living conditions, and to surrender it to said representatives for return to the organization if the conditions are found unsatisfactory.

8. To assume all responsibilities for this dog's actions, including any damage done by this dog.

9. To keep this dog as my pet and household companion. To ensure that when outside and unattended, the dog is in a secure fenced yard or kennel run with adequate shelter from the elements. To exercise him or her on leash or within a fenced yard or run, and never to allow the dog to run loose without adequate adult supervision. To never chain or tie this dog without being in attendance.

10. To never allow this dog to be transported in the open bed of a pickup truck or similar vehicle without being properly secured in accordance to law.

When you have read and signed the contract or the terms of adoption, the rescue group will countersign it and you will both receive a copy. You will also receive any pertinent information you will need before bringing the dog home, such as dates of vaccinations and the type of food the dog has been eating. You will also need to pay the adoption fee at this time.

The rescue volunteer will make an appointment to meet with you to actually transfer the dog. If your home is not yet ready, wait until you have everything you need prior to picking up the dog. It's best, too, to wait until you will be home for a few days so the dog won't come to a strange house and then be left alone. So, check your calendar, and make an appointment with the rescue group for your dog's homecoming.

•••••••••••••••••••••••••••••••••••••••

CHAPTER 5

BEFORE YOU BRING YOUR NEW DOG HOME

Before you bring home your rescue dog, you will want to take a close look at your house and yard and verify they are safe. Your new dog will not understand that your residence is going to be his new home. He may be worried, stressed and may misbehave. He may also try to run away. So dog-proofing everything is going to be very important.

You will also want to establish relationships with some pet care professionals. A veterinarian will be needed to help you maintain your rescue dog's good health, and a groomer will teach you how to care for your dog's skin and coat. You will also want to start your rescue dog in a training class shortly after you bring him home, so find a trainer you will trust.

Chances are that even if you already have a dog, you will need to go shopping prior to bringing your new dog home. Go through the checklist that appears later in this chapter and see what you will need.

DOG-PROOFING YOUR HOME

One of the biggest mistakes many dog owners make is they give their dog (particularly young or newly adopted dogs) too much freedom. Most people realize that young puppies will get into trouble; that's a given! However, many rescue dogs have never been taught house manners; in fact, many have never been allowed in the house. They have no concept of correct house manners and will chew on things and destroy things without understanding those behaviors are unacceptable. By limiting your dog's freedom when he's inside, you can prevent problems while teaching him the rules of your house.

Confining your dog in the home not only prevents your possessions from being ruined, it helps keep your new dog safe. Dogs don't realize that chewing on an electrical cord can shock and kill them; they just see this thing dangling in front of their nose that looks like it would be fun to put in their mouth. They don't understand that oven cleaner is deadly; it smells pretty interesting to them. Making your house safe for your new dog is very important.

In the rooms where you will allow the dog to run around (under your supervision, of course) get down on your hands and knees and look at things from a dog's point of view. Are there magazines that could be chewed up? Pick them up and put them away. Books on the bottom bookshelf? Those would be fun to chew. Cords dangling from behind the television, DVD player and stereo? Remote controls on the sofa end table? Go through the rooms and put away everything valuable, chewable or dangerous that is within reach. You'll be amazed—this will include an incredible amount of stuff.

Before your dog comes home, have everyone in the house get into the habit of putting away possessions, picking stuff up and closing bedroom or closet doors. When living this way becomes a habit, the house becomes much safer for the dog. Make sure, too, that everyone in the house understands the new rules. If someone leaves their slippers on the floor and they get chewed up, it's not the dog's fault. Until he's been taught the house rules, and really understands them, he just doesn't know any better.

DANGEROUS STUFF

Keeping your dog safe means he will be around longer for you to love and for him to love you. Our homes are full of dangerous things.

SOME FAVORITE DOG CHEWABLES

Electrical cords   Books and magazines
Telephone cords   Shoes and socks
Remote controls   Children's toys
Cell phones   Medicine bottles
                            Food, dishes, cups and utensils

EMERGENCY INFORMATION

If you think your rescue dog has eaten something potentially poisonous, immediately call the National Poison Control Hotline at 1-800-222-1222 or the ASPCA Animal Poison Control at 1-888-426-4435.

Make sure all of these things are put away and safely out of your dog's reach.

Around the house: cigarettes, pens and felt tip pens, many different houseplants, laundry products and hobby supplies.

In the home office: paper clips, push pins, staples, computer cords and mouse.

In the kitchen: oven cleaners, floor cleaners and wax, bug sprays, insect traps, furniture polish and dishwasher soaps and rinses.

In the bathroom: medicines, vitamins, bathroom cleaners, toilet bowl cleaners, some shampoos and conditioners, hair coloring products and many cosmetics. Don't forget the toilet scrub brush.

In the garage and yard: car maintenance products, including oils, gas and antifreeze, fertilizers, weed and insect control products, snail and slug bait, mouse and rat traps and baits, paints and paint

Make sure your house is safe before you bring home your dog.

removers. If you have a pool, many of the treatment products are also dangerous.

Dog-Proofing Your Yard

You need to dog-proof your yard just as you did your house. Make sure the kids' toys are put away, the gardening supplies are out of reach and the pool chemicals are stored in a safe place. Assume, just as is true indoors, that if anything is left within reach, the dog will chew on it.

Look at the yard from your dog's point of view. Can he get under the deck and is it dangerous if he does? Are there any vents attached to the house that he could crawl through? Does the television cable go into the house inside the yard? If so, are the cables exposed? There are many things in the backyard that are potentially dangerous, and the yard offers many ways in which the dog can be destructive.

Inspect the Fence

Your yard is going to be brand-new to your rescue dog and he will be curious. If there is a hole in the fence, your rescue dog will stick his nose in it, and if he can make the hole bigger, he will. He may not want to actually go anywhere, he's just curious about what is on the other side of the fence.

Be aware that some rescue dogs are quite insecure and may try to escape. Make sure the fence itself is sound and all holes—even tiny ones—are covered. It may be a good idea to run hardware cloth (wire fencing) over the inside of the fence, from the ground to about three feet high. Make sure there are no holes under the fence, either. If there is a gap between the ground and the fence, your dog can dig well enough to get under it.

If you feel your fence might not be secure or that your yard has too many dangers, build your new dog a dog run. A fenced area, four feet wide by 12 feet long, is more than sufficient for most dogs. If you are adopting a toy breed dog, the run could be smaller, and if you are adopting a larger breed dog, make it bigger.

Make sure that the run is escape-proof, with no gaps between the ground and the bottom of the fence, and if you are adopting a breed that likes to climb (Siberian Huskies and Beagles, to name just two!) make sure the dog run has a top. Place the run in a spot where the dog has access to some shade at all times of day. Provide the dog with a big bucket of water and a few toys. The toys will make the run seem like a fun place to spend time rather than an unpleasant confinement or form of punishment.

DANGEROUS PLANTS

Many common landscaping plants are dangerous. Some will just make a dog nauseous but others are toxic. The plants listed below are some of the most common yard and garden plants in this country; however, plants used in landscaping vary from region to region. If you have any doubts about the safety of the plants in your yard, talk to a horticulturist or a poison control center. As the saying goes, "It's better to be safe than sorry!"

PLANTS TO AVOID

Amaryllis	Hemlock
Avocado (leaves, not fruit)	Horse chestnut
Azalea	Hyacinth
Belladonna	Iris
Bird of paradise	Jasmine
Bottlebrush	Lily of the valley
Boxwood	Milkweed
Buttercup	Morning glory
Calla lily	Mushrooms
Common privet	Oleander
Crocus	Pennyroyal
Daffodil	Poison ivy, oak and sumac
Dieffenbachia	Rhododendron
Dogwood	Sweet pea
English ivy	Tulip
Foxglove	Yew

CALLING IN THE PROS

Dog owners do not—and should not—try to cope with dog ownership alone. Why suffer through bad behavior when a trainer can help you change it with much less hassle? Why teach your dog to hate being brushed when a groomer can show you how to easily get rid of tangles? Let professionals help you; that's why they do what they do!

Usually, the most reliable way to find a good professional is through personal referrals. If you ask several dog owners which veterinarian they recommend and one name keeps popping up, well, that vet would probably be a good choice. Yellow Pages ads are fine; coupons in the mail are okay, but keep in mind anyone can place an ad. On the other hand, pet owners who have relied upon pet professionals can tell you about firsthand experiences.

The rescue group from which you are adopting your dog may be able to give you some referrals, too. In fact, many pet professionals offer discounts to dogs adopted through a rescue group. So ask your rescue group volunteer for some recommendations, and when you talk to these professionals, inquire about possible discounts.

When you have a few referrals, make an appointment to meet with each one. They may ask you to pay for their time, but if they do, please remember that their time is their livelihood! When you meet with a professional, be ready with your questions. These might include:

What are their business hours?

What are their payment procedures? Do they have any financing for emergencies (especially the veterinarian) or do they accept credit cards? Which ones?

Is the veterinarian familiar with health problems rescue dogs might face? Or dogs of your breed?

Is the groomer comfortable working with dogs of your breed?

Does the trainer understand the housetraining difficulties faced by an adult dog? Do they like working with your breed?

By interviewing and selecting a few pet professionals before you bring your rescue dog home, you'll have an immediate, familiar resource to turn to when you need it.

DOG SUPPLIES

Okay, so your house is dog-proofed and your yard is safe for a dog (or you have set up a dog run). You have found a few pet professionals you feel comfortable with, and you have a rescue dog on the way. What else do you need? How about some dog food? Food and water bowls? A leash and collar? Your rescue dog is going to need some supplies, so let's get an overview of the must-haves.

You will want two bowls of appropriate size for food and water. I prefer big water bowls that are difficult to tip over or spill, as I've had several dogs who liked to play in the water. However, if you are adopting a Yorkie or a Papillon, be sure to get a bowl from which he can reach the water! Ceramic or metal bowls are usually best; plastic bowls often turn into chew toys!

Make sure you have some food on hand that the rescue dog is used to eating. If you want to change to another brand, do so gradually. Changing your dog's diet right away will give him a bellyache and diarrhea. Take two to three weeks to switch foods. The first week, feed three parts of the old food with one part of the new food. By the end of the first week and first part of the second, combine the portions so that one-half is old food and one-half is new. By the end of the second week to the beginning of the third, move to one part old food to three parts

CANINE CABINET SHOPPING LIST

Dog food (the kind he's used to eating)
Food and water bowls
Leash
Collar
Identification tag
Toys
Crate
Brush
Clean-up supplies
Baby gate

of the new food. This will get the dog accustomed to the change gradually and ease any gastrointestinal upset.

Your rescue dog may come to you with a collar and leash. If he doesn't, you will need a soft nylon buckle collar for everyday use. Once you begin training, your trainer may recommend a training collar. Don't buy one yet; wait for class and find out what type of collar they recommend. For going on walks, you will need a leash right away. A nylon or leather leash, four to five feet long, is great for most dogs.

Have a collar identification tag ready when your dog comes home, with your telephone number on it. You can always get a new one later with the dog's name on it too. Most pet supply stores have equipment that can engrave the tags while you wait. Eventually, you will want to talk to your veterinarian about having a microchip injected under the skin at your rescue dog's shoulder. (The rescue group may already have done this. Many do.) This is a permanent identification and is recommended by most pet professionals and animal control officers.

Your rescue dog will need toys! Active, curious, intelligent dogs need stuff to keep them busy and if there are no toys to play with, a non-toy will suddenly take on a whole new purpose! Balls, toys that make noise, toys designed for chewing, and food-dispensing toys are all good choices.

Some rescue dogs have never learned how to play and do not understand what toys are, so these will be fun activities to introduce him to. I'll discuss some good dog toys later. Right now just make sure you have a few different toys to make available.

You will need a crate for your dog, and in upcoming chapters, you'll get all the details about how and why to use a crate. For now, just understand that the crate is an awesome training tool for your new dog. It will help with housetraining, with preventing many problem behaviors, and it also serves as your rescue dog's bed and special place.

In a nutshell: The crate should be big enough for the rescue dog to stand up, turn around, lie down and get comfortable—and no larger. There are three basic types of crates: plastic, heavy-gauge wire and soft-sided. Which you choose is up to you. You may want to ask the rescue volunteer if your new dog has been crate trained and if he has, what type of crate he is used to.

Your new dog will need some grooming supplies, although what you need will depend primarily upon what breed of dog you are adopting. Talk to the groomer you like prior to going shopping for grooming

NOT YET BEDTIME

Don't buy an expensive dog bed right away. Wait until the dog is grown up, settled into your house and well housetrained. At first, a few washable old towels will work just fine.

supplies. Not only can they help you choose the right tools, but they may recommend some specific brands available in your area. They may also be able to get you some tools at a discounted price. It doesn't hurt to ask!

Don't go overboard and buy out the grooming shop; just get the basics and add to these as you need them or as your groomer recommends.

You will want to have some white vinegar on hand for cleaning up the inevitable housetraining accidents. Paper towels, a scrub brush and trash bags are necessary, too. Save your plastic grocery bags for picking up after your dog while out for a walk. You will probably also want a pooper scooper for cleaning up feces from your yard.

Baby gates were designed to keep human babies and toddlers safe, but they work just as well for dogs. Baby gates can close off rooms and block off hallways so that your dog cannot sneak off somewhere to have a housetraining accident or chew on your shoes. Garage sales are a great place to pick up playpens or baby gates.

With the above items, your dog pantry should be pretty well stocked. Let's go get that dog!

• •

CHAPTER 6

THE BIG MOVE

.

Your new dog's rescuer or foster owners have probably told you quite a bit about her. But if you still have questions, ask them before you pick up the dog. Find out: What words does she understand? Dinner? Supper? Hungry? Biscuit? Cookie? Go potty? Ball? Toy? The more you know about your dog, the easier the transition will be.

WHEN YOU PICK UP YOUR DOG

Make an appointment to pick up your dog on a day when you can spend the rest of the day with her, and preferably, will have at least a weekend with her as well. It's not unusual for newly adopted dogs to have some anxiety or even fear when first taken to a new home, and you will want to be there with her to calm those fears.

One or two other family members can come with you to pick up the dog, but don't take all three kids, two of their friends and Grandma. That would be entirely too much excitement and confusion. Keep this outing quiet and calm.

When you pick up your dog, have an appropriately sized crate with you. Not all dogs ride nicely in the car and you don't want to have an accident because your dog is throwing herself around the inside of the vehicle. An old towel folded on the bottom of the crate is a good cushion and is easily washed in case of a housetraining accident or motion sickness.

Greet your new dog in a friendly, but calm, manner. If you make a big fuss, you could overwhelm her. After you take care of any necessary paperwork, simply walk her to your car, ask her to jump in, crate her and leave. Don't have any long good-byes with the foster owners; don't drag out the questions with the rescue group volunteers. That will only make things more stressful for your new dog. Keep it short and sweet and as drama-free as possible. You can always call them later if you need to.

Go straight home with your dog. This is not the time to run errands. She is probably worried anyway and any delays will only compound that anxiety.

THE FIRST HOUR AT HOME

Leash your dog as you take her out of the crate and walk her into the yard or house on leash. Far too many dogs escape from their new owners before even making it into the house. (Not on leash and worried about her new situation, the dog runs off when the car door is opened. This is not the scenario you want to start off with.)

Before the family greets her, take the dog outside to relieve herself. Give her the command her foster family taught her to go potty. When she's done, bring her in to meet the family.

Have everyone sit in the family room or living room, and give each person some dry dog food or dog treats. Tell everyone to be calm and quiet, to watch television (not too loud!) or read, and to ignore the dog. She will be confused by people calling her and begging her to come to them. Instead, let her go approach family members on her own. When she does go to someone, they can give her a bit of food, pet her and talk to her. If she is reserved, tell everyone to leave her alone. Let her watch things and relax.

Note: Baby gates should be set up before you pick up your dog. Don't let her wander down hallways or sneak off somewhere. You want to prevent any potential problem behaviors (including housetraining accidents) so keep her in the room where you and your family are.

IF YOUR DOG TAKES OFF

If something does happen and your new dog runs away at any time, perhaps through an open door or over the backyard fence, call the rescue group immediately. Your dog's foster owners might be able to coax her back; after all, she knows them. The group might also have microchipped the dog and they can notify the local animal control or humane society. Cooperate with the rescue group as much as you can while they coordinate efforts to find the escapee.

How your dog reacts initially to your family will depend upon many things, including her personality and temperament, how well she was socialized, and how she was treated by her previous owners. If she is by nature happy, extroverted and stable, and was well loved by her first family, she should interact well with yours. If she is cautious and reserved with strangers, and was not well socialized as a puppy, it may take her some time to relax.

In addition, dogs of some breeds tend take a little more time than others to get comfortable in new environments. Sarah Filipiak, president of Pound Rescue of Athens, Ohio, said, "German Shepherds may take a few weeks to bond with their new owners, depending on their previous surroundings or how long they were in foster care." Breeds that were designed or bred to be protective, cautious, reserved or stand-offish usually take a while to adjust to new family members.

After an hour or so, let family members return to their normal routine but keep loud noises and roughhousing to a minimum for a few days. Let the dog follow people around, watch what's going on, and get adjusted to the everyday household activities and schedule. Family members can talk to her, offer to throw a ball, and pet her, but make sure no one is forcing her to accept unwanted petting or affection.

At this point, too, make sure everyone in the household understands how important it is to keep doors closed and latched, gates locked and garage doors closed. Make sure the dog is on a leash when outside of the fenced yard. If your new dog panics and runs at this point, she doesn't know where her new home is and she doesn't know you yet. You could potentially lose her forever.

WHAT'S HER NAME?

Your rescue dog probably has a name, but she may not. And if she was rescued as a stray or from a shelter, her name may be unknown. Sometimes it's a good idea to change her name in any event, as this gives the dog a fresh start.

So think about it. Do you like her name? Does she seem to like it? When you say her name, does she perk up? Does her tail wag? Is her name a happy thing to her? Or has her name been used in punishment? Does she duck her head and tuck her tail when she hears her name? If it is apparent to you that your dog's name does not elicit a positive reaction from her, by all means give her a new one.

If you want to change her name (for any reason), do so now as she joins your family. Choose a name that you can say with a happy tone of voice. It's tough to say "Killer" with a smile, but it's easy to smile as you say "Bubbles!"

Introduce her name to her by saying it with a smile in your voice as you look at her, pet her, encourage her to play and as you rub her tummy. Say her name often. When she begins to look at you as you say it, praise her. "Bubbles! Good girl, Bubbles!"

Keep her new name positive. Don't say her name if she's in trouble for something she did. In those instances, just say, "Bad girl!" Use her name in happy situations or in training, but not for corrections.

THE FIRST FEW DAYS

Let your new dog get to know your family and household routine for the first few days. Don't force her to get involved in household activities, just let her watch and follow people. She may be grieving for her owners or foster owners. She may be worried, or shy, or confused. Just allow her to observe, and when she does begin to participate, don't make a big deal out of it.

Every dog is different and how each dog reacts to a new situation will vary. If a friend adopted a Greyhound who settled in immediately, with no adjustment worries, don't necessarily expect your new Greyhound to be the same way. Each dog is an individual and needs to find her place in her own time.

INTRODUCING YOUR RESIDENT DOG

A new dog in the home will invariably upset the social structure perceived by the resident dog. To make the transition as stress-free as possible, introduce your new dog to your resident dog outside, preferably in a neutral area such as a local park. Have both dogs on leash and ignore them as much as possible while keeping an eye on them. Keep leashes loose and be as casual as you can. If a dog growls, turn her away and distract her for a few minutes. (Don't inadvertently praise or reward the growling, however!)

When things seem calm and the dogs are not paying much attention to each other, swap leashes and dogs. If you were holding the resident dog and your spouse was holding the new dog, switch dogs.

Repeat the same exercise. When the dogs are calm and relaxed, bring out a toy and let them play while keeping the leashes on in case you need to separate them.

When the dogs seem comfortable (to the extent this happens during the initial meeting), bring them home together. Keep the leashes on in the house for a while. Keep all activity calm and low-key; if either dog gets too excited or over-stimulated, separate them for a while.

EASING THE ADJUSTMENT

The first week or so after joining your household is quite stressful for your new rescue dog. She is in a new home filled with unfamiliar smells, new people and maybe even other pets. The schedule or routine is probably even different from her original home and her foster home.

Don't expect your new dog to love you right away. She will need to learn to trust you first, love will follow. Let her come to you, both physically and emotionally. Just be available and when she does

It takes time for a dog to adjust to new owners and a new home. Be patient.
Soon your dog will be part of the family and you won't be able to imagine life without her.

approach, remain calm but welcoming. In other words, respond to her favorably but not so enthusiastically that you scare her away.

Let your dog follow you around the house as you tend to daily chores. Try to keep her with you as much as you can, but let her spend time outside in the backyard, too. If she is with you constantly, when you do have to leave her to run errands or go to work, she may panic. She needs time to bond with you, yet also needs time alone to learn that you will still be there later.

Let your dog adapt to the schedule of your household. Dogs are creatures of habit and a schedule is security. Let her learn when she will eat, when she will go outside, when you both will go for a walk and when you leave the house without her.

Make time every day for some exercise. Exercise is a great stress reliever (for you and your new dog)! A good jog, a fast-paced game of Frisbee or game of catch with the tennis ball are all good for shedding some of the nervous energy that comes with a new situation. It will also give you a chance to play with your new dog; to laugh and giggle at bad throws and awful catches, to cheer good catches and to enjoy each other's company.

BEDTIME!

Where is your dog going to sleep? You don't want her wandering off to have a housetraining accident, nor do you want her to chase your cat in the middle of the night. It will be hard to prevent these events if she's sleeping on your bed, so that is not a good choice. But she shouldn't sleep in the laundry room or garage either. That's too far away.

Your dog needs to be close to you, yet confined so she doesn't get into trouble. The ideal situation for most dog owners is to place the dog's crate in the bedroom with them. (Chapter 9 discusses crate training in detail, including how to choose the right crate for your dog and how to introduce your dog to the crate.) The crate will quickly become your dog's bed, her refuge and her own special place. Later, when she is adjusted to your home, fully and reliably housetrained, and you know she won't get into trouble at night, you can take the door off her crate. It can still serve as her bed, but she can come and go as she pleases.

WHEN AND WHERE TO FEED

Your dog needs to know when she will be fed, and you should make every effort to maintain that schedule as closely as humanly possible. If she's eating twice a day (morning and evening) select times when you will be available every day.

Feed her in a spot that is neither completely isolated nor too busy. If she's all alone she may not eat; feeling she is being punished. If the area is the center of activity, she may be too distracted to eat, or she may gulp her food too quickly out of fear that something will happen to it. A corner of the kitchen may work well or perhaps a spot in the family room. Look around your house and choose a place that will suit both your dog's needs and your own.

ESTABLISH SOME HOUSEHOLD RULES

Although you don't want to place too many demands upon your new dog too soon, you also don't want to let bad habits develop. You can introduce some household rules on her first day home, just do so gently and with guidance rather than harsh corrections. Show your dog what to do, help her do it, and prevent as many undesirable behaviors as possible.

Do you want your dog up on the furniture? I like to cuddle with my dogs so my dogs are allowed on the furniture. I protect my sofa with a blanket or afghan and have the dogs lie on that. However, many people don't want the dog up on the furniture and that's perfectly acceptable, too. So make a family decision and then stick to it.

HOUSE RULES

For the majority of dog owners, the dog is not allowed to:
    Jump on people.
    Wander through the kitchen sniffing for food.
    Raid the trash cans in the house or outside.
    Dash through any open door or gate.
    Chase the cat or other pets.

Do you want to allow your dog up on the furniture? Decide now and enforce the rule consistently.

Housetraining is, of course, one of the most important household rules. You want your dog to learn where to go to relieve herself, how to ask to go outside and when to do it. Chapter 9 will discuss housetraining the adult dog in greater depth, however, right now just take the dog to the spot where you wish her to relieve herself. Tell her to go potty and praise her when she does. Take her to this area often in the beginning and don't let her have free run of the house; keep her close to you. You don't want accidents to happen in out-of-the way parts of the house.

Where is the dog to be allowed to play? I prefer to keep my dogs quiet in the house, as I have more than one dog and more than one cat. If things get rowdy, my house could be trashed in a heartbeat. So my dogs are encouraged to play outside. Inside, they can bounce around and carry toys or chew on chew toys but all rough play is discouraged. However, if you have a bigger house or only one dog, you may want to encourage inside play. It's your choice. Just make a definite decision and make sure everyone in the family understands it.

When establishing household rules, think about what would make your dog a more welcome family member and then teach your dog to do those things (or not do unpleasant things). It is very important that all family members agree to, and follow, these household rules. If one person in the home encourages the dog to get up on the furniture, but no one else allows it, the dog will be confused and her behavior will never be consistent.

PATIENCE AND CONSISTENCY

The keys to the first days and weeks with your new dog are patience and consistency. Be patient with her as she gets to know you and other family members. Be patient as she learns the schedule and routine of your home and its residents. Be patient when she makes mistakes; after all, this is all new to her.

Be consistent as you teach your new dog the rules of your household. Be consistent about housetraining, about sitting prior to going in- and outdoors, and about getting up on the furniture.

With patience and consistency she will learn and adapt, and will become the member of your family that you dreamt of.

CHAPTER 7

• •

BUILDING A RELATIONSHIP

Dogs provide us with companionship, fun, laughter and security. Dogs provide opportunities for socialization and are a tie to the natural world. But these gifts, and so many more, are provided to dog owners by their pets if, and only if, the dog is able to bond with the owner and the other members of the family.

WHAT IS BONDING?

There are many definitions of the term *bonding,* especially as it applies to domestic animals and their people. But the easiest way to understand bonding is to view it as a process. It is the process whereby a dog and owner make an emotional connection. When your dog looks to you for leadership, guidance and affection, and when you look at your dog and smile, you have bonded.

Many dog owners, particularly those who have grown up with dogs and other pets, or who have had pets all their adult lives, seem to bond naturally with animals. These lucky people may think the process happens on its own and doesn't require any thought. And for them it may occur naturally; they don't have to think about it. But for people new to pet ownership or for people with their first companion dog, knowing *how* to bond with a dog can further the process.

Time together is the first requirement for bonding. You need to be able to spend time with the dog right away. You can't say, "Oh, I'll have time next month." That's too late. So when you bring your new dog home, plan on having *at least* a weekend with him and then at least some time each and every day for the first few weeks.

You don't have to do anything special during this time other than be with the dog. Although it's fun to spend time playing with the dog, walking him and grooming him, your time together does not have to be assigned, or allotted, or filled with activities. You can also let him hang out with you in the yard as you rake, or prune trees or garden. You can let him follow you around the house as you clean. Just spend time with him, talk to him, acknowledge his presence and be happy to be with him.

The next step in bonding is getting to know each other. You need to know what all those funny personality quirks are that everyone (dog or human) has. How does your dog react when you say the word "treat" or "play"? Does he like Frisbees so much that he'll spin in circles when he sees one? Does he like to go to bed right at 10:30? Is he a morning dog, waking up happy, smiling and joyful? Or is he a slowpoke in the morning? As you get to know your dog and get to know all the nuances of his personality, you will begin to develop an affection for him. Whereas you may have liked him the first time you met him, now that relationship will deepen and develop into a more lasting affection. This is a part of the bonding process for you.

While you are getting to know your dog, your dog is also watching you. He is discovering all the funny quirks of your personality, too. He may find that you have a sore spot for dogs digging in the garden; that this will make you yell. He may also discover that you have a soft spot for big brown eyes and that you will stop whatever you are doing if he looks at you with eyes wide open. You may think your dog is just following you around the house and yard, but in reality, he is studying you! And this, too, is a part of the bonding process.

Your dog will need to spend time with other family members so he can bond with them, too. When your son comes home from school, encourage him to spend time with the dog, to throw the Frisbee in the backyard or keep him with him when he's in the house doing chores. Your daughter can have the dog with her in the backyard while she's playing or in her room with her while she's doing her homework.

ONE-PERSON DOGS

Some people brag (or complain) that their dog is a "one-person" dog. Very few dog breeds were bred to be one-person dogs. Instead, this situation is created by a lack of socialization or by preventing the dog from bonding with other people.

BONDING'S UNPREDICTABLE ELEMENTS

You may make a connection with your dog faster than your dog will to you. If your dog was bonded strongly with his previous owners, and is still grieving for them, he may not take to you right away. When this happens, you may feel disappointment, as if the dog doesn't like you. But please, don't take this personally, give the dog time. He'll come around. Because he has bonded with and loved people previously, he will miss that closeness and he will then bond even more strongly with you.

Dogs of some breeds tend to bond more slowly than others. As a rule, the working and herding dogs bond strongly to their owners and take that bond seriously. They often grieve horribly when separated from their owners. If they are introduced to new owners when grieving, the new bond can be slow in coming. German Shepherds, Australian Shepherds, Belgian Malinois, Bouvier des Flandres, Saint Bernards and Rottweilers, to name just a few, are very attached to their owners. These dogs can bond with new owners and will be just as dedicated to their new owners as they were to their first; it may just take some time.

Some breeds are known for adjusting to their new homes very quickly. Greyhounds, especially retired racing Greyhounds, always seem very grateful to have a new home and seem to settle in quickly. Boxers, English Springer Spaniels, Papillons, Japanese Chins and Shih Tzus are happy, joyful dogs and usually bond quite readily to new owners.

ESTABLISH YOUR LEADERSHIP

As you and your dog begin to bond and get to know each other better, it's time to start establishing your leadership. Dogs, as social animals, need a leader who provides guidance and security. As your dog's new owner, that becomes your job.

Some very simple behaviors can help make you a leader in your dog's eyes. First, carry yourself like a leader. Stand tall. When you pet your dog, lean over him to pet and hug him. Do not kneel on the ground or sit on the floor and hug your dog at his level and thereby allow him to stand over you. In your dog's language, a dog demonstrates dominance by putting a chin or paw on the subordinate dog's shoulder. Don't put yourself in the subordinate dog's position.

A leader is kind, caring, fair and firm. A leader demands respect but is not overbearing or harsh. A leader enforces the rules but is not violent or abusive. A leader wields his power softly, but is not apologetic or cringing.

Don't fawn over your dog. Talk to him, carry on a conversation with him, smile at him and pet him when he's done something right, but don't pet him too much. If he has a more dominant personality, he may think all that excessive petting is his due. He may think you are submissive because you are giving him all this extra attention.

In Chapter 6, I discussed establishing some household rules. As the leader, you need to enforce those rules. If you don't want your dog on the sofa, don't let him up on the sofa. When he hops up, tell him "Acck! Get off the sofa!" and make sure he does get down. When he goes to his blanket instead of the sofa, praise him, "Good boy!"

Obedience training helps establish you as your dog's leader, too. The type of training you do—the technique you use—must be suited to both your personality and your dog's. There is a variety of techniques available; from all-positive training to more compulsive techniques. I'll discuss these in more detail in Chapter 10, but at the onset, it is important to begin some basic obedience training.

Teach your dog to sit for everything he wants. Have him sit before he gets a treat, or his dinner. Have him sit before you throw the ball or the Frisbee and have him sit before you hook up the leash to take him for a walk. Have him sit when he greets you. When you have him sit, he learns to work for you (he sits for you, he gets a treat!) and he learns self-control. (A dog who is sitting for petting can't jump on you and ruin your clothes.)

When trying to establish yourself as a leader, think about the best boss you ever worked for. She was probably a fair yet firm boss while still being friendly and approachable. You always knew where you stood with her. Pattern your leadership skills after that boss. If there were aspects of her leadership you didn't like, feel free to change those in this relationship. Just remember, in your dog's world, affection must be balanced with respect.

YOUR DOG'S PAST

Your dog's past does have an influence on his relationship with you today and in the future. Although dogs don't dwell on the past, they do

Teach your dog to sit. This is the foundation command for everything else you teach him.

react to things because of prior treatment and experiences. So your dog's ability to bond with you, develop a relationship with you and even live comfortably with you are all affected by what happened to him before you came into his life.

The first few weeks of your dog's life set the tone for his future relationships. If your dog's mother was accidentally impregnated and her owners (although negligent for not having her spayed) were angry about the puppies, they may have been rough with the puppies or may not have handled them at all. These events could cause the puppies to grow up with a fear of people.

The foundation for a dog's socialization to people, other dogs and other animals is laid when he's a young puppy. Puppies need to see and meet kind people of all ages, sizes and ethnicities. They also need to meet cats, rabbits, sheep and other animals as well as friendly dogs of all sizes and shapes. If this socialization does not happen, or is mismanaged, your dog could be fearful of strangers or potentially aggressive toward strangers.

ALL ABOUT COMPROMISES

Living with a rescue dog is all about compromises. Every dog has a history over which you have no control. You have to learn what undesirable behaviors you can change, and what undesirable behaviors you can live with.

When you adopt a dog, you may be able to get some information about his formative months from the dog's first owner, "Yes, we got Max from a good breeder, and we socialized him carefully as a puppy. He went to the pet store with us to meet other dogs and we took him to a puppy class." Or you may not get any information at all.

Other types of past events can be related to your dog's behavior today. If he was hit with a broom, he may carry a fear of sticks and brooms with him forever. If he never heard a big loud trash truck before (perhaps his owners lived in a rural area) he may be afraid of trash trucks. If he was locked outside in the backyard alone the first time a thunderstorm came overhead, he may be panic-stricken during thunderstorms.

You'll probably need to do some detective work to determine where your new dog's idiosyncrasies lie. Try to avoid letting your dog get the impression that you are as scary as someone was in his past. And don't try to make him face all his fears right away. There's plenty of time for that later. Right now just understand that his past does have bearing on his present and future, and try to understand that his behaviors have nothing to do with you personally.

DO STUFF!

Building a relationship shouldn't seem like work. Even though you should consciously put energy into the relationship building, take time to have fun with your dog, too. After all, most of us get dogs because we enjoy their companionship.

Take your dog for car rides. As long as the weather is cool enough, he can go with you as you run errands. If the weather is warm, just take him places where he won't be left in the car. (A car can heat up to *deadly* temperatures in as little as five minutes.)

Enroll in a basic training class and when you graduate from that, enroll in a fun class, such as agility, flyball, Frisbee or therapy dog volunteer work.

Go for walks in different places. Walk around the local boat harbor, watch the seagulls and smell the salt air. Hike in the hills, look for deer and enjoy the wildflowers. Walk in different neighborhoods; even at the local flea market. The more varied your dog's experiences, the better equipped he becomes to cope with new ones.

Check out different regional parks where dogs are allowed. Explore new walking trails and see if you can find a new place for a picnic or for overnight camping.

Introduce him (carefully and without coddling him) to new things. Let him see and hear a motorcycle go whizzing past. Let him sniff a pet rabbit. Let him follow a shopping cart. Let him see, smell and hear the world around him and as he does, let him know that you are with him to make sure that everything is okay.

CHAPTER 8

• •

INTRODUCING THE DOG
TO YOUR WORLD

As your dog bonds with you and your family, you will want to begin introducing her (gradually!) to your extended family, your neighbors and friends. How quickly you acquaint her with new people will depend upon her personality. Not only does she need to learn where things are in the house and yard, she needs to learn where she is in the neighborhood, and learn the sights and sounds of the area. She will need to be introduced to the pets in your family, too, including the cat, rabbit, ferret, bird and any other pets. Socialization is an ongoing process.

THE IMPORTANCE OF SOCIALIZATION

Socialization is the continual process of introducing a puppy (or in your case, a dog) to the world around her. When a puppy experiences a variety of people, places, things and events in the world around her, she develops skills that allow her to cope with that world. When a motorcycle zooms past, a well-socialized dog may look, cock her ears, process that information—"Ah-ha. I've seen those before"—and will continue walking. A dog who has not been well socialized may react with panic, pulling on the leash while trying to run away, or worse yet, she may try to slip out of the leash. She may bark and growl at the motorcycle or react negatively to those around her since she can't get to the motorcycle.

A dog who has been socialized to the sights, sounds and smells of the world around her learns to think (instead of react) when things happen. She develops confidence in herself and trust in you that you are there to help her.

Once your dog has adjusted to her new home,
a group training class can be great socialization.

Although your rescue dog is probably not a puppy, you can still socialize her and much of this socialization can be as simple as allowing her to meet new people. Take her outside and introduce her to your neighbors. Let her meet the neighborhood kids; the retirees down the street and the teenagers two doors down. Let her meet people of all ages, sizes, shapes and ethnic backgrounds.

You will want to have your dog at home with you for at least a week before you do a lot of socialization. After all, she needs to bond with you and your family first. However, once she's comfortable with you, then start taking her outside to meet the neighbors. Gradually increase her socialization as she appears to be ready for it.

You can also plan outings so that she can go different places and meet other people. Walk in a park, along the river, by the beach and in the hills. Walk in urban areas and in rural areas when possible. Visit your friends in their apartment complex and bring her with you in the elevator.

Many businesses are great opportunities for socialization. An ice cream store, pizza place or even a tire store all have people coming in and out; most of whom will want to meet your dog as you wait outside on the sidewalk.

Take your dog to family get-togethers. Let Grandma, Grandpa, aunts, uncles and all the kids pet her and play with her.

Take her to the pet supply store with you. Let her meet the sales clerks as well as other customers and then reward her by letting her pick out a new toy. In the pet store, she can also learn how to walk on slippery floors and see things she wouldn't see at home (such as display shelves and stacks of aquariums). She can also learn to walk next to a shopping cart—something that is very different!

One of my favorite socializing techniques is to take a dog to the veterinarian's office—even when she doesn't have an appointment. Just walk her in, have the receptionist pet her and give her a treat and then leave again. To the degree possible, you want the vet's office to be something special instead of something scary!

SEE, SMELL AND HEAR

Introduce your rescue dog to as many things as you can; not all at once, of course, but gradually. As she becomes more familiar and comfortable with the world around her, her confidence will grow.

While protecting her from harm (and without reinforcing fear) let her see, hear or smell the following:

In the house:

The vacuum cleaner

The dishwasher, garbage disposal and trash compactor

The washing machine and dryer

The hair dryer

A plastic garbage bag being shook open

A paper bag being crumpled

A broom and mop being used

A plastic bag being popped

A metal cookie sheet being dropped to the floor

Children's toys, including some that make noise

Balls of various sizes, shapes and colors

Outside:

A car engine being revved

The trash truck out front

A motorcycle zooming down the street

People (and kids) on bicycles, skateboards and inline skates

In the backyard:

The lawn mower

A weed whacker and leaf blower

A rake being used

The hose being shook out, untangled and curled up again

Water coming from the hose (but not squirted at her!)

Metal and plastic trash cans, including the lids

In addition, you can help to acclimate your rescue dog to different surfaces by:

Walking her up and down some stairs

Walking her over a wooden footbridge

Walking her over a metal manhole cover

Walking her on carpet, artificial turf, slippery floors and rubber matting

KEEP IT HAPPY!

The key to socialization is to introduce your rescue dog to the environment without frightening her. That means your tone of voice should be happy and upbeat; it should sound like someone just offered you an ice cream cone: "Ice cream!"

If your dog reacts fearfully to something, do not "save" her. If you hug her or coddle her, or say, "It's okay, sweetheart, don't worry," she will take all that reassurance and assume you are praising her for her

> ## ONE STEP AT A TIME
>
> Don't try to introduce your dog to everything all at once. Overwhelming
> her is just as bad as not socializing her. This should be a gradual process,
> taking place over the first few months of her life with you.

fear. In other words, you would be telling her in human terms not to
be afraid, but in her canine terms, she would be hearing that she was
right to be afraid. This is a common misunderstanding.

To avoid this type of miscommunication, be very upbeat. When
something startles her, say in an "ice cream" tone of voice, "Wow! What
was that?" and when you can, walk her up to the "scary" thing. "Here
look at this." Touch the motorcycle, or flapping sheet on the clothesline
or the child on the skateboard. Encourage her to come close and sniff
the scary thing or person and when she's brave, praise her!

WHEN SOCIALIZATION ISN'T WORKING

If your dog was not socialized as a puppy, if her socialization did not
continue on into adulthood or if she has a tendency toward aggression
or fearfulness, your socialization efforts may not work. She may lunge
and growl and even snap at other people or other dogs.

Displays of aggression shouldn't happen too often with rescue dogs,
as most groups do have screening procedures to weed out potentially
dangerous dogs. However, dogs are dogs and sometimes unpredictable;
especially in a new situation.

Should you find your dog acting aggressive or overly fearful, call a dog
trainer or behaviorist who is used to working with rescue dogs. And call
right away. Don't wait until the dog has bitten someone or has attacked
another dog. Call the rescue group from which you adopted the dog, too.
The volunteers need to know about troublesome behavior problems.

INTRODUCING OTHER PETS

In Chapter 6, I discussed how to introduce your new dog to your resident dog. You may have other pets who your dog needs to meet and
learn to respect.

Cats present a challenge to dogs who have previously chased them. I hope that during your pre-adoption interviews, you asked the rescue volunteers whether this dog is good with cats. At home, introduce your dog to the cat with the dog on leash. Should she lunge toward the cat, use the leash to stop her and tell her in a firm, no-nonsense voice, "No! Leave the cat alone!" Do not allow the dog to be off leash in the same room with the cat until you know (*really* know) that she will not chase the cat. Praise her when she looks at the cat but does not chase it. I like my dogs to believe that the family cats are superior to them in the "social hierarchy" of my house. This way, the dogs do not chase or otherwise harass the cats.

Ferrets are also a challenge to some dogs. They move quickly, make chirpy noises and move sideways. Nothing else looks, smells and bounces around quite like a ferret! Introduce the dog to the ferret just as you did the cat. Keep the dog on leash and let the ferret bounce around. If the dog lunges, correct her just as you did when she lunged toward the cat. Again, when she looks but doesn't dash, praise her. When the ferret is in its cage, don't allow the dog to torment the ferret. No biting at the cage and no barking. The cage is off limits, too.

UNSOCIAL EVENTS

To prevent your dog from developing a fear of children (or to prevent the exacerbation of whatever fear she may have) ask them *not* to:

- Run around the dog. This could be frightening or over-stimulating.
- Scream and yell while playing with the dog. Again, this is over-stimulating or scary.
- Grab your dog's head or body and hug her.
- Throw themselves on top of her.
- Grab her face, put their face in hers, blow in her face or stare at her.
- Get rough with your dog for any reason, even in play. Although kids are the most likely group to engage in these behaviors, the above rules apply to adults too. If people won't heed your request, take your dog and walk away.

Rabbits, hamsters, pet rats, other rodents and birds are a particular problem for many dogs because in the wild, these animals are prey. Sporting dogs are particularly attracted to birds and terriers to the rodents, but any dog of any breed can find these creatures intriguing. Keep these pets securely caged and teach your new dog to ignore the cage. If you will be playing with these small pets, put your dog outside, or after she's had some training, have her do a down/stay. But, even with training, be very careful.

Don't expect your dog to be best friends with your cat, rabbit or bird. Dogs and cats can be good friends, eventually, but this takes time. The cat will need to learn to trust the new dog and the dog needs to learn restraint around the cat. So be cautious and be patient with them.

INTRODUCING YOUR HOUSE AND YARD

You may not think your new dog needs to be introduced to your house and yard; after all, she is living there, right? Nonetheless, she may not really know them yet and you need to introduce her to her surroundings.

In the house, begin by having her follow you around. She should be doing that anyway as a part of her bonding with you. Just take her all over the house. Let her smell your son's room full of computer stuff and dirty clothes and let her walk through your daughter's room of sports gear and craft supplies. Take her through the laundry room and garage.

As you're walking, keep going back to the family room or the room where your dog has spent most of her time. What you want her to learn is how to get around. If she gets left in your son's room, does she know how to get to the back door to ask to go outside? This may *seem* very simple, but to a dog new to your house, it can be confusing and frightening.

Do the same thing in your backyard if you have a big, or oddly shaped yard. My backyard, for example, is C-shaped. The dogs go outside through the garage, which has a dog door. They then walk down the side yard, which is long and narrow, to the backyard. A new dog may not be brave enough to venture all the way to the backyard and may stop in the side yard. Because I like the dogs to relieve themselves in the backyard, this would not make me happy. So walk your dog back and forth a few times.

COMFORTABLE WITH YOUR WORLD

The whole idea behind socialization and introducing the dog to your world is to make sure your dog is comfortable with her surroundings. If she is afraid, or shy or doesn't understand what's going on, she isn't going to be at ease. As a result, she won't be a particularly good companion. So show her your world.

CHAPTER 9

HOUSETRAINING
YOUR RESCUE DOG

Most people assume an adult dog will be housetrained and in many cases that is true. Rescue volunteers know, however, that many of the dogs going through a rescue program are not as well housetrained as one would like.

The perfectly housetrained dog is one who will not have accidents inside, will ask in some manner to go outside when he needs to and, preferably, will relieve himself in one spot outside. Ideally, the dog will also understand a command to relieve himself, and then can do so when needed by his owner, especially when on walks, when visiting or traveling.

Unfortunately, many rescue dogs are given up by their owners because of housetraining problems. In addition, many dogs given up for other reasons have housetraining problems, too. Some otherwise house-trained dogs have adjustment problems with either their new foster home or new adoptive home, and they demonstrate those adjustment problems by having a lapse in housetraining manners. So, housetraining is often a concern for the rescue dog owner.

DON'T ASSUME ANYTHING!

When you bring your rescue dog home, don't assume he is house-trained. Even if his former owners said he was housetrained or his fos-ter owner said, "He was pretty good," don't assume anything. Instead, work under the assumption that you need to train him. By doing so, you can prevent accidents from happening and you can prevent dam-age to your floors and carpets. In addition, if you have adopted a male dog, you can prevent or stop leg lifting (which is the male's way of making your house his!).

Housetraining an adult dog is very much like housetraining a puppy except that the adult dog will usually progress faster in his training. Notice I said "usually." If your dog has been housetrained previously, or even partially housetrained, he will most likely be trustworthy within a few weeks. Baby puppies, on the other hand, must be supervised for several months. Other than the amount of time it takes to train the dog, the process is very much the same.

THE BENEFITS OF A CRATE

A crate (often called a kennel or a kennel crate) is a travel carrier for dogs. Originally designed for dogs being transported on airplanes, it is now also used to help dogs learn housetraining skills. A crate works by utilizing the dog's own instincts to keep his bed clean. Very few puppies or dogs will soil their bed so they learn (with your assistance) to not go in their bed and to relieve themselves where you wish them to go.

There are three types of crates available and each type has its advantages and disadvantages. You need to look at your needs and the needs of your dog, and choose which crate would work best. The most popular type of crate is made of plastic or fiberglass. It has a metal, barred door and barred windows for ventilation on each side. Plastic crates come in two parts, top and bottom, and are easily cleaned. They are relatively lightweight and although somewhat bulky, are easily stored. Because they have solid sides, plastic crates provide the dog with a feeling of security; much like a den.

PET STORE DOGS

If your rescue dog was originally bought from a pet store, he may have trouble learning crate training. Because pet store dogs spend too much time in a cage, they must relieve themselves in the cage. They in turn lose their inhibition about soiling their bed.

Heavy-gauge wire crates are more like a cage. The open sides provide good air circulation, and in hot weather, they're wonderful. Because they are open, though, some dogs feel exposed and vulnerable. These crates are heavy, although most brands do fold up flat for carrying and storage. They usually have a metal tray in the bottom that can be pulled out and removed for cleaning.

The third type is often called a carry bag rather than a crate but it is essentially a soft-sided crate for carrying toy breed dogs, cats, ferrets and other small pets. These can be very useful for transporting your toy breed rescue dog to the vet's office or groomer, but these should not be used for daily training. With the soft sides, these crates collapse too easily, can be chewed through and do not provide enough security for you or your dog.

Choose a crate that will allow your dog to stand up, turn around and stretch out. Too much room is not better. If the crate is too big, the dog can relieve himself in a back corner and still have room to get away from it. The purpose of using a crate to housetrain your dog is to utilize his instinct to keep his bed clean.

The crate will become your dog's own personal space. It is a place where he can hide his favorite toys or bones. He can retreat to his crate when he's tired or doesn't feel good. He will sleep in his crate at night and will spend some time there during the day when you are unable to supervise him.

The crate should never be used for punishment. Never put your rescue dog in his crate as you are scolding him. Never yell at him or berate him while he's in the crate; not only will these episodes make him think the crate is a bad place, but those types of corrections are not good dog training techniques.

INTRODUCING AND USING THE CRATE

You are going to want your rescue dog to think the crate is a fun place all of his own, so how you introduce him to it is important. Place the crate in the living room or family room and fasten the door open so it cannot close unexpectedly and startle your dog. Have a few dog treats and toss them one at a time toward the crate. Let your dog grab and eat those treats. A little while later, toss a treat or two into the crate and let him get those.

DO NOT OVERUSE THE CRATE!

Other than at night, do not leave your rescue dog in the crate for more than a couple of hours at a time. During the day, he needs time to stretch his legs, run and play. If you and other family members work all day, make some arrangements for your dog. Perhaps you can ask a neighbor to take him out and walk him. Many teenage kids will walk dogs for a few dollars a week. If you can't make other arrangements, then a secure, safe, covered dog run might be the best answer.

When he will go in and out with no trouble, start feeding him in the crate but continue to keep the door open. When he will eat in the crate with no fuss, close the door behind him. Do *not* let him out if he throws a fit! Open the door only when he is calm and quiet. If he cries, barks and scratches at the door, ignore him.

Put the crate in your bedroom at night so your rescue dog can hear you, smell you and be close to you all night. This is eight hours of closeness that you couldn't find the time for at any other time of day. Rescue dogs need time with their owner and these seven to eight hours each night don't require you to do anything except sleep; but to your dog, these hours are wonderful.

In addition, with the dog close to you, you can hear him if he gets restless and needs to go outside. If he doesn't have to go outside and is just moving around, you can reach over, tap the top of the crate and tell him, "No! Quiet!"

During the day, put the dog in his crate every so often; whenever you are too busy to supervise him. Because he has to spend many hours in his crate at night, try to keep his time in it during the day to relatively short periods. Thirty minutes here and there are okay as long as he gets plenty of attention, exercise and time with you as well.

PREVENTING PROBLEMS

A crate can assist you in preventing your dog from learning bad habits. When you can't supervise your rescue dog, put him outside in a safe place in the yard or put him in his crate. By ensuring he doesn't get into trouble, you are preventing problem behavior. He will never learn that it's fun to chew up the leather recliner if he never gets a chance to do it! By preventing the bad behavior, you can also ensure the dog learns good habits. The dog learns to chew on the toys you give him rather than learning to be destructive.

THE HOUSETRAINING PROCESS

Housetraining doesn't have to be difficult. In addition to using the crate, you will also need to limit your dog's freedom so he doesn't sneak off to have accidents. You will also teach him what you want and where you want it and that you will set a good schedule. It's not that hard! Really!

TAKE YOUR DOG OUTSIDE

Take your rescue dog outside where you want him to relieve himself. Stand outside with him but don't interact with him. When the dog starts to sniff and circle, just watch. After he has started to relieve himself, tell him softly, "Go potty! Good boy to go potty!" (Using, of course, whatever terminology you wish to use. But be aware that once your dog learns your elimination command, that is what he'll respond to. You don't want to develop a habit of using words you couldn't say in public if you had to.) When he has completed his business, praise him even more.

DOG LITTER BOXES

Litter boxes for tiny dogs have been in use for many years. Most dog owners used cat boxes of a larger size, complete with either cat litter or dirt. However, in the past few years, commercial dog litter boxes have become available (a little bigger and deeper than cat boxes) complete with litter made specifically for dogs. These work well for toy breed dogs in apartments, or toy breed dogs left alone while the owner is working.

USING THE "GO POTTY" COMMAND

It is important your rescue dog understands his command to relieve himself. If you take the dog to go visit someone, it is very nice to be able to tell the dog to relieve himself before going inside the house. The same concept applies when you're traveling. If you stop to get gas, you can then tell the dog to relieve himself, and even if the bladder isn't full, he can try.

You will need to go out with him to that particular spot every time he needs to go for several weeks. Yes, weeks! You cannot simply send the dog outside. If you do, how do you know he has done what he needs to do? How can you teach him the command if you aren't there? And how can you praise him for doing what needs to be done if again, you aren't there? Even worse, if you let him back inside when he hasn't relieved himself, it's then your fault if he comes in and has an accident.

Housetraining is a very important skill, and many dogs (including many rescue dogs) end up at animal control shelters because they haven't been well housetrained. Take your time with your rescue dog and teach him correctly; it's too important to rush.

ROUTINE IS IMPORTANT

Dogs, like many people, are creatures of habit. Housetraining is much easier if the dog eats, sleeps and goes outside on a fairly regular schedule. Variations are allowed, of course, but not too many.

Keep in mind that a very young dog or a dog with medical conditions may need to eat two to three times per day. He will need to go outside to relieve himself after each meal. He will also need to go outside after playing, when waking up from a nap and, in the beginning of his housetraining, every two hours in between.

Take all of these things into account when you set up a schedule. Take into consideration, too, your normal routine. You may have to make some adjustments in your typical practices to get the dog outside often enough. But a little personal sacrifice goes hand in hand with having a dog!

A sample schedule may look like this:

6 A.M.: Dog goes out as soon as he's let out of the crate.

7 A.M.: Take him outside again after he eats breakfast.

9 A.M.: It's been two hours.

11 A.M.: It's been two hours and he's just woken up.

1 P.M.: It's been two hours.

3 P.M.: This outing can be canceled today because he was out on a walk.

5 P.M.: He's outside playing.

6 P.M.: Outside after eating dinner.

8 P.M.: Outside after playing with your son.

10 P.M.: Last trip outside before going to bed.

As your rescue dog's training progresses, he will be able to go longer between trips outside, but this ability will grow over time.

WHEN YOUR RESCUE DOG'S GOTTA GO!

Once you have set up a schedule for your rescue dog, you need to get him outside. In addition, you want to teach him to notify you when he needs to go out.

When I have a dog at home, I use my voice a lot as a training tool. As I walk the dog toward the back door, I will ask him, "Max, do you have to go potty?" in a high-pitched, happy tone of voice. As the dog reacts to my tone of voice and as he learns the words, he will get excited and dash toward the door. I will praise him for that. I will praise him again when he relieves himself in the proper place outside.

As the dog gains more control and can go longer between trips outside, I will check with him once in a while, "Do you have to go potty?" If he does, he will dance and wiggle and head toward the door. I will, of course, praise him and let him out. If he just stares at me, that means he doesn't need to go right now, thank you!

Later, as they get older, my dogs will come and stare at me when they want my attention. When I turn to look at them, they will tell me they need something. Dax will stare, turn toward the door and look back at me as if to say, "Follow me, Mom!" Riker puts his head in my

> # NO BARKING, PLEASE!
>
> I do not teach my dogs to bark to go outside because as a dog trainer, I hear many complaints about barking dogs. Teaching a dog to bark to go outside can be encouraging a potential behavior problem..

lap. I will then ask the dog, "Do you need to go potty?" If the answer is yes, then I will let the dog outside.

It takes time and maturity for the dog to learn to ask you for help. Some rescue dogs don't want to leave the people in the house long enough to go outside and so try and hold their bladder too long. You have to remember the dog's schedule and make sure he gets out in time.

NO EXCUSES!

Many rescue dog owners seem to be masters at making excuses. I don't know if it is because their dogs may have been in a bad situation previously, but excuses are always readily available. "He had an accident because he ate too much!" or "It is too cold/hot/windy/rainy/snowy outside." As a dog trainer, I know very well that excuses will not housetrain your dog.

COPING WITH ACCIDENTS

Now, I understand that accidents will happen. Perhaps you won't be watching the dog closely enough and he will urinate on the floor. When an accident does happen you must handle it very carefully. It is important the dog learns that urinating and defecating are not wrong but the place where he did it was wrong. If the dog feels that relieving himself is wrong, then he will become sneaky about it and you will find puddles in strange places all over the house. Now you have a real problem.

If you come upon the dog as he is having an accident, then use a verbal correction, "Acck! What are you doing?" Scoop him up and take him outside. Then clean up the mess but do not let him watch you clean it up. If you find an accident after the fact, do not correct the dog—it's too late.

Don't rub the dog's nose in his mess—that teaches him that the urine or defecation *causes* the problem and that's not what you want him to learn. Don't drag him to his mess and shake him or yell at him; that will only confuse him. Remember, the act of relieving himself is not wrong; it is the act of relieving himself *in the house* that is wrong. Make sure your message is very clear.

If your dog is having a few accidents in the house, you need to make sure you are going outside with him so that you can praise him when he relieves himself outdoors. Be certain he knows when and where it is right. You will also need to pay more attention to the dog's schedule; are you getting him outside often enough and at the right times? You may also be giving him too much freedom. If he isn't reliably house-trained, make sure he stays in the room with you and cannot head off to another room.

Successful housetraining is based on setting the dog up for success by allowing few accidents to happen and then praising the dog when he relieves himself outside.

SHOULD YOU INSTALL A DOGGY DOOR?

A doggy door is a small door (or flap) that permits your rescue dog to go in and out as he pleases without any assistance from you. Doggy doors can be very effective for adult dogs who are left home alone for many hours each day. The dog can go outside to relieve himself or to lie in the sun yet can get back inside when he so desires.

A doggy door can be great, but do not rely on the doggy door to replace your participation in the training process. Door or no door, you are a vital part of it. You need to go outside with your dog to teach him the command to relieve himself. You also need to praise him when he does relieve himself in the correct place. If you go out with him most of the time, and allow him to go out by himself once in a while, the doggy door can work.

One problem with the doggy door is, you don't know whether your dog has relieved himself. If you are getting ready to take him for a car ride, do you know whether he has a full bladder? Even with the door, you still need to go outside with him often.

Submissive Urination

Does your new dog urinate a little when you greet him? Or when strangers greet him? Does he produce a puddle when you scold him? Although some dog owners call this a housetraining accident, it really isn't. This is submissive urination and is a leakage of urine connected with having a strong emotion. Some dogs do it when they are being scolded, others do it when they're very happy and others leak at any strong feeling.

Do not scold your dog for this! Scolding or punishment will only make the problem worse. After all, it's caused by emotion, right? Scolding causes more strong emotions!

Instead, work on building your dog's confidence. Some training and fun games will help. Your fair leadership will help boost his confidence. After he has been with you a while and his confidence level continues to rise, you will see a marked decrease in submissive urination. One day you will remember, "Hey, he used to leak!" and realize it hasn't happened in quite a while.

A Physical Problem

If you have followed all the guidelines for housetraining and nothing seems to work; or if your dog suddenly seems to have forgotten his housetraining; take him to see his veterinarian. A bladder or urinary tract infection or other associated problems often lead to accidents. Some rescue volunteers feel that 15 to 20 percent of all housetraining problems in rescue dogs may be health related. Those figures may be high, but keep them in mind should housetraining problems continue, or resurface.

Be Patient

Be patient with your dog's housetraining. Establish a schedule that seems to work for you and your dog and stick to it. If you follow the right schedule and limit your dog's freedom, your dog will do fine. However, the lack of accidents doesn't mean you can back off on your supervision; instead, a lack of accidents means your training is succeeding! If you ease up too soon, your dog will have some accidents and you'll have to start all over again. All your efforts will pay off when you find that you have a well-housetrained, reliable dog.

CHAPTER 10

ALL RESCUE DOGS NEED SOME TRAINING

All rescue dogs need some training. Not only will training in the basic obedience skills teach your dog the household rules that are important to you, but the process itself will help develop and cement your relationship. As you learn how to teach your dog, you will get to know her better and in turn, she will learn what you expect from her. Training will also help build her self-confidence and that is very important for dogs who may still be grieving for former owners.

The eight basic commands discussed in this chapter will teach your dog important skills that are fundamental to desirable conduct at home with you and out in public. Some of these commands teach your dog self-control; to be aware that there are consequences to her actions. She will learn that if she does what you ask of her and restrains her desires to run and jump and play (at least for the moment), she will be praised and rewarded. If she doesn't restrain herself, there will be no praise or rewards, and depending upon the actions and situation, there could be consequences.

In other situations, the command may serve as an alternative behavior to prevent problems. For example, your dog cannot jump on people if she learns to sit for praise and petting. She cannot pull your arm out of the socket, dragging you down the street, if she learns to walk nicely on the leash while watching you.

Any training you decide to do later with your dog rests on these basic commands. She will need to understand these thoroughly before she can go on to any advanced training or any dog activities or sports.

TRAINING TECHNIQUES GALORE!

There is a standing joke among dog trainers. Ask 100 dog trainers a variety of questions relating to training, and the only thing they will agree on is that their technique is the best and all the other trainers are wrong! Unfortunately, this is true. All trainers have their own way of training. No one method is always right or always wrong as long as the method is humane and fair to the dog.

The method I'll be describing is a balanced training system. It emphasizes the positive and sets the dog up to learn and succeed. This method also shows you how to teach the dog when she's made a mistake and then how to teach her to do what it is you want her to do. This method is easy for most dog owners to learn and is effective on many dogs. However, if you have a method that you prefer more than this one, fine! As long as it is easy for you to do, and is fair and humane for the dog, that's great.

You and your dog should enjoy your training sessions.

TEACHING THE SIT

Teaching your dog to sit is relatively easy. Teaching her to sit still is a little harder, but I'll take this in small steps and together we will set her up to succeed. With your dog on her leash close to you, show her a treat. When she reaches up to sniff the treat, move it over her head toward her tail as you tell her, "Bubbles, sit." When her head comes up and back to follow the treat, her hips will go down. After she sits, praise her and give her the treat.

If she spins around to try to get the treat rather than sitting, put the treat away in your pocket. Put one hand on her chest where the chest and neck meet. Tell her, "Bubbles, sit," and at the same time, push that hand slightly up and back (thereby pushing her chest up and back) as the other hand slides down her back toward the hips and tucks her hips down and under. Think of a teeter-totter; up and back at the chest and down and under at the hips. When she's sitting, praise her.

You want your dog to understand that the word "sit" means "put your hips on the ground, keeping your front end up, and be still." Now obviously you cannot tell your dog this and expect her to understand, so you must teach her that's what it means and you can do this using your voice. When she does sit, praise her with a higher than normal tone of voice, "Good girl to sit!" When she begins to move from position (not after she's gone) but when she begins to move, use a growling tone of voice, "Acckk!" and put her back in the sit position.

The sit is a very useful command, not just as the foundation for more advanced commands but also for use around the house.

Have the dog sit to greet people especially if she likes to jump up to greet them. She can't jump on people and sit at the same time.

Have her sit when you fix her dinner; she can't jump on you and knock the bowl out of your hands when she's sitting.

Have her sit when you hook up her leash to take her outside. If she's sitting, she can't be spinning around in circles out of excitement.

Have your dog sit for everything she wants. Have her sit for petting, for her dinner, for treats and for toys.

When she comes up to you and nudges you to pet her; have her sit first. When she drops her tennis ball at your feet; have her sit first. By teaching her to sit for everything she wants, you are establishing behavioral rules, giving her structure (which is important for every dog), and you are giving her a job to do. Don't forget that most of the breeds of dogs were originally bred to do a job of some kind. For a pet, this job is no longer being pursued and the dog misses the activity and the stimulation. Sitting for everything she wants can be your dog's first job!

TEACHING THE RELEASE

Once your dog is sitting, what do you do then? Do you just let the dog get up? How does she know when she's done with the sit? The release is a command that means, "Okay, you're done now, you can move." With this command, the dog knows exactly when she's allowed to move from position.

Begin with your dog sitting, then pat her on the shoulder as you tell her, "Okay!" in a high-pitched tone of voice and encourage her to get up from the sit by raising your hands high. If you lift your hands up and bounce a little yourself, she will probably bounce up, too, copying your movements.

The primary purpose of the release command is to let the dog know when she is free to move from a previous command. This alleviates confusion; she knows when she's done.

TEACHING THE DOWN

As with the sit, your dog already knows how to lie down. And as with the sit, teaching her to move into the down position and then being still can be a little harder!

Have your dog sit. With a treat in one hand and another hand on the dog's shoulder, tell her, "Bubbles, down," as you let her sniff the treat. Take the treat directly to the ground in front of her front paws. (Lead her nose down with the treat.) As she starts to move down, the hand on her shoulder can be assisting her in this downward movement. However, don't push! If you push, she may simply push back. When she's down, give her the treat and praise her.

If your dog watches the treat move toward her paws and doesn't follow it, try this technique. Again, begin with your dog in a sit. Tell her "Bubbles, down," as you gently scoop her front legs up and out, laying her down. You can do this by reaching over her shoulders with one arm to grasp the front leg away from you while your other hand grasps the closest leg. Gently lift both legs up, forward and then down.

The down command is very useful, both in the house and out in public. You will use the down in conjunction with the stay command; which I'll describe next.

Have the dog lie down during meals so that she isn't begging under the table. Place her where you can see her but away from the table.

Have her lie down at your feet while talking to guests. She can't be jumping all over them or knocking their drinks over if she's still at your feet.

Have her lie down and give her a toy to chew on when you would like to have some quiet time to read or watch television.

Have her lie down while you're talking to a neighbor.

Have her lie down while you get your mail out of the box and sort through it.

When your dog is in the down position, she can relax. Because she is relaxed, she can then hold it longer than she could a sit.

TEACHING THE STAY

The stay command is used with the sit and lie down commands. You will want your dog to understand that "stay" means "remain in this particular position while I walk away, and remain here until I come back to you and release you." The sit and lie down commands by themselves teach the dog to hold that position until you release her; but only while you are with her. With stay, you will be able to walk away from her.

Begin with your dog in a sit. Hold your hand in front of her face about two inches from her nose and tell her, "Bubbles, stay!" Take a step or two away. If she moves, use your voice, "Acckk!" and put her back in position. Wait a few seconds and then step back to her. Have her hold still while you praise and pet her, and then release her with the release command.

If she is having a hard time holding still when you step away, try this technique. Again, begin with your dog in a sit. Hold your hand in front of her nose and tell her, "Bubbles, stay!" But this time, in one hand hold the leash up from her neck behind her head, without holding it tight. Take a step away while you continue to hold the leash up. If she moves, tell her, "Acckk!" as you give her a gentle snap and release correction with the leash. Use only as much snap and release with the leash to get her attention and no more. Put her back in position. Wait a few seconds, then step back to her, praise her and then release her.

After practicing the stay with the sit, try it with the lie down. The training methods are the same except that you will be having the dog lie down. However, you tell the dog which to do. If you ask her to

USING THE SNAP AND RELEASE

Although most of us would prefer to train our dogs using only positive, reward-based techniques, many dogs (especially those with established bad habits) need to know what it is that they are doing wrong. If you use a snap and release of the leash to let your dog know when she's making a mistake, use only enough "snap" or force to get her attention. The snap should be an attention-getting tool; *not* a punishment. The snap should always be used with a verbal correction: Snap and release and "Acck! No jump!" Never tighten the leash and keep it tight; never choke your dog; and never, ever lift her off the ground using a tightened leash!

sit/stay and she decides to lie down, correct her and help her back up in to a sit. She doesn't get to choose which exercise; you do.

Don't be in a hurry to move away from your dog or to have her hold the stay for longer time periods. It is very difficult to hold still and right now it's more important that your dog succeeds in her training.

Use the stay around the house in conjunction with the sit and lie down.

When guests visit, have the dog lie down by your feet and tell her to stay. She cannot then be tormenting your guests!

When you want her to stay away from the table while you're eating, have her lie down and tell her stay.

Tell her to sit and stay while you're fixing her dinner so she doesn't jump all over you and spill her food.

Have her sit and stay at doorways, gates and at the curb so you can teach her to wait for permission to proceed.

There are lots of uses for these commands. Just look at your house, your routine and where you might be having some problems with your dog's behavior. Where can the stay help you?

TEACHING THE COME

The come is a very important command; one that could potentially save your dog's life some day. When I teach my dogs to come when called, I want them to understand that come means "stop what you're doing and come back to me right now, with no hesitation, as fast as you can run." This instant response might save your dog from a dangerous situation, such as being attacked by an aggressive dog or a snake, or being hit by a car.

Take a small plastic container, like a margarine container, and put a handful of dry kibble dog food in it. Put the top back on. If you shake it, you will hear a nice rattling sound. With your dog sitting in front of you, have the shaker in one hand and some good treats in the other. Shake the shaker and then pop a treat in her mouth. Hard dog training! You are building a relationship in your dog's mind between the sound stimulus (the shaker) and the food treat. Essentially you are telling your dog the sound of the shaker equals a treat. Obviously this means you need to use a treat your dog really likes! Practice this for two or three times and then quit for the training session but come back to it later and do it again.

After two or three days of this training, start with your dog sitting in front of you, shake the shaker, say, "Bubbles, come!" in a happy tone of voice and then pop the treat in her mouth. Now you're changing the equation. Now the sound of the shaker equals the word "come," which equals the treat popped in her mouth! Practice this for several days, two or three times per session.

When you find your dog sitting in front of you with her mouth open, waiting for the treat, start backing away from the dog as you say "Bubbles, come!" Lead her by the nose with the treat as you back away. After a few steps, pop the treat in her mouth and praise her, "Good girl to come!"

In a week or two, depending upon how enthused your dog is, you can stop having her sit in front of you when you begin. Instead, when she's across the room from you, pick up the shaker, call her and when she charges across the room to you, praise her and pop the treat in her mouth.

Using the sound shaker helps your dog focus on the sound of the word "come." Rescue dogs have problems with the come with some frequency; either they were never taught well or the command was used to punish them. Perhaps your dog chewed on something, her previous owner called her to come and then punished her. They meant to punish her for chewing, but in her mind, the punishment is related to the last thing that happened. In this case, the last event was coming to her owner! Confusion!

However, because you will initially teach her that the sound shaker equals a good treat, and then the shaker equals the word "come" and a treat, you'll change the whole idea behind the word and hence, the command.

Because the come command is so important, I urge you to teach it using two techniques. For this second technique, have the leash on your dog, hold the leash in one hand and have some treats in the other. Back away from your dog as you call her, "Bubbles, come!" Make sure you back up a few steps so she gets a chance to chase you. If she doesn't come to you right away, use the leash to make sure she does. Praise her when she approaches you, "Good girl to come!" Later, you can practice this using a long leash.

As your dog learns the come exercise and is responding well to it, add some games to the practice. Using two shakers, call her back and forth between two family members and offer her a treat each time she comes. Make sure you keep it fun and exciting.

TEACHING THE WATCH ME

Training your dog can be very difficult if you can't get your dog to pay attention to you. When you tell your dog to "watch me," you want the dog to look at you, your face—preferably your eyes. The dog is to ignore any distractions and focus on you. At first, this focus may only last for a few seconds, but later, as the dog gets better at it and as her concentration gets better, she should be able to focus on you and ignore distractions for minutes at a time.

Begin with your dog sitting in front of you. With treats in one hand, tell your dog, "Bubbles, watch me!" Let her sniff the treat in your hand and bring it up to your chin. This movement and position are important. Let the dog sniff the treat so she knows you have it. Take it up to your chin (slowly) so that as she watches the treat, her eyes follow your hand to your face. As she looks at the treat and then your face, praise her. After you praise her, "Good girl to watch me!" then pop the treat in her mouth. If she gets distracted and looks away, take the treat back to her nose and get her attention back to you.

As the dog learns the command, you can start making it more challenging. Tell your dog, "Bubbles, watch me!" and then back away from her so that she has to watch you while walking. When she can follow you for a few steps, back up in a zigzag pattern, making turns and corners. Back up quickly, then slowly. Add some challenges. Of course, when the dog can do this, and has fun following you, you should praise her enthusiastically!

TEACHING "LET'S GO!"

Good on-leash skills are necessary for all dogs. When on leash, the dog should respect the leash without fighting it, pulling on it or choking herself on it. The "let's go" command will help teach those abilities.

Start with your dog on the leash. Tell her, "Bubbles, let's go," and simply back away from her. If she watches you, praise her. If she follows you, praise her even more. However, if she sniffs the ground, looks away from you or tries to pull in the other direction, use a snap and release of the leash and a verbal correction, "Acckk! No pull!" (Or "no sniff," if that's appropriate.) After the correction, if she looks back up to you, praise her.

Remember, the snap and release should be just powerful enough to get her attention and no more. The snap and release is not a punishment. Use it just to get her attention so you can use your other training tools (voice and treat) to teach her.

Back away from the dog several times in different directions. Each time she follows you and each time she looks up at you, praise her. Every time she pulls away, sniffs the ground or ignores you, correct her.

Your goal is to have your dog keep the leash slack as she follows you, paying attention to your every move. And of course, when she does, you will praise her enthusiastically!

TEACHING THE HEEL

You want the command "heel" to mean "walk by my left side with your neck and shoulder area next to my left leg, maintaining that position no matter what I do." With that definition, if you walk quickly, jog, walk slowly or simply amble, your dog should stay with you at your pace. If you go for a walk through a crowd and have to zigzag through people, your dog should still maintain that position.

Learning the heel, however, requires a great deal of concentration on your dog's part. Do *not* start teaching the heel until your dog has been doing the "watch me" for several weeks (not days, weeks!) and has been doing the "let's go" very well for at least two weeks with regular practice.

*If you find you enjoy training, you might want
to look into dog sports such as agility.*

Always practice heeling with your dog on leash. Hold the leash in your left hand and some treats in the right. Back away from your dog as you tell her, "Bubbles, let's go!" As she follows you, let her catch up with you as you back away slightly and turn so that you are facing the direction you'll be walking and she ends up on your left side. Walk forward together as you show her a treat and tell her, "Bubbles, heel!" Stop after a few steps, have her sit and praise her as you give her the treat.

Repeat this several times, keeping each walking session short, enthusiastic and fun. Make it challenging by turning, walking quickly, walking slowly and going in different directions.

At this point in the training, with this technique, always start with the "let's go!" command and tell the dog to heel as she arrives at your left side and you begin walking forward together. This way, you are starting with two known commands and your dog knows what to do when you give them. As you are moving and your dog is in position, you then give the new command, "heel."

Once you have been practicing this for a while (maybe two weeks) begin by having your dog sit by your left side. Hold the leash in your left hand and have some treats in your right hand. Show the dog a treat and tell her, "Bubbles, watch me!" When she's paying attention to you, tell her, "Bubbles, heel!" and walk forward. If she pulls ahead, use the leash to give her a snap and release correction as you tell her, "Acckkk! No pull!" When she slows down, backs off the pulling and looks back to you, praise her and repeat the "watch me" command. When she watches you, praise her enthusiastically.

As she gets to know this command, make the heel practice more challenging. Don't simply walk in a straight line; that's boring for both of you!

USE THESE COMMANDS

Use these commands in your daily life with your rescue dog. The commands will work best when you *use* them. If you only use the commands during your practice sessions, your dog will believe that's what they are for. What you want your dog to understand, instead, is that these are new rules for day-to-day living.

Take a look at the examples listed in this chapter, and find ways to begin incorporating the commands into your daily routine. This shouldn't be hard to do. Your rescue dog may be resistant initially; after all, these activities may be new and different. Moreover, she has probably been training *you* and may be getting comfortable with this modus operandi. However, with some practice and some motivation, she will get into the new routine, too.

PRACTICE, BUT HAVE FUN

All of these commands need to be practiced on a regular basis. After all, the only way your rescue dog will know them well and do them reliably is through practice. But practice can also be boring, so make the effort to keep your training upbeat, fun and different. Practice in different places. Use different training treats. Keep your voice upbeat and happy when you praise your dog. If it's fun for you it will be fun for her. You can both have fun and still pursue your goal of having a well-trained, reliable companion.

CHAPTER 11

•••

WORKING THROUGH PROBLEM BEHAVIORS

My oldest dog, Dax, is a barker. She likes to warn me whenever someone is in front of our house, near the cars or approaching the gate. I
don't mind when she reacts as a watchdog; in fact, it gives me a feeling
of security; no one will ever sneak up on our house! However, I don't
want Dax to bark when the neighborhood kids are playing out front—
especially when they are nowhere near our driveway! Nor do I want
her to bark when the mail carrier stops at a neighbor's house. It has
taken some time and training to teach Dax when she is allowed to bark
and when I want her to remain quiet.

Unfortunately, many rescue dogs have some problem behaviors.
Some, like Dax, are over-protective and must learn some limits. Some
rescue dogs like to jump up on people, some dig up the back flower
garden and others like to raid the trash can for treasures. Many of these
problems are manageable, but it seems that many dog owners do not
understand this. Problem behaviors are a large cause of the number of
dogs that are turned over to shelters and rescue groups every day.

NOT PROBLEMS TO YOUR DOG

Most dog behaviors that humans consider problems are not problems
to the dog. Dogs bark because they have something to say; they are
communicating just as we speak. Dogs dig because the ground smells
good or because they are after a gopher. Dogs chew because it's fun or
because they're teething. They raid the kitchen trash can because there
are wonderful tidbits in there. All of these things are natural actions to
the dog; they are not problems to him! But there are other factors, other

than the sheer pleasure that the dog gets, that contribute to problem behavior; sometimes quite significantly.

IS YOUR DOG HEALTHY?

Bad behaviors are usually triggered by something. If your dog has been well housetrained and suddenly begins having accidents in the house; make an appointment with your veterinarian. Often a urinary tract infection will cause housetraining accidents. Other health concerns can also serve as a catalyst for problem behavior, so a thorough exam is always a good idea.

Medications can have side effects that show up in behavior. If your dog has recently started a new medication and his behavior has changed, talk to your veterinarian.

When you make your appointment, and at the time of the visit, be clear with the veterinarian that you want to consider health problems that might be connected with unwanted behaviors. Don't just ask for an exam and leave the vet guessing as to why they're examining your dog!

ARE YOU THE LEADER?

Dogs lacking leadership can develop a host of behavior problems, such as leg lifting, marking, mounting and humping. Aggressive behavior toward family members is common, as is destructive behavior around the house. Food guarding, toy guarding and similar behaviors are also seen with frequency in dogs who do not have a strong sense of their proper place in the family hierarchy.

Most (but not all) dogs have a desire to please and are more than willing to grant you the role of family leader. However, a rescue dog with a dominant personality, particularly one who does not feel the leadership from his owner, may try to assume the position. In your rescue dog's eyes, if you are not the leader, someone must take on the role!

FEELING WELL AND ACTING WELL

A number of dog behaviorists and trainers feel that at least 20 percent of all behavior problems are related to the dog's health in some way.

WARNING!

If your rescue dog is an adult and thinks he's the leader, you will want to change his understanding of your relationship. But do so carefully. If you even *think* you could be bitten, hire a trainer or behaviorist to help you. Don't wait until a bite happens!

If you have not yet convinced your rescue dog you are in charge, you need to change how he regards his (and your) position in the family hierarchy.

Some ways to enforce your role as the boss include preceding your dog through doorways and gates. You go up and down stairs before he does. Make him wait for you to take the lead.

Make him sit for everything he wants. Give him one (and only one) command to sit and then help him do it.

Have him lie down and stay at your feet (while you are either sitting or standing) at least twice per day.

Feed him at set times, giving him his food and taking it away after fifteen minutes. Do *not* free-feed, leaving food out all the time. You want to clearly establish that you are the decision-maker.

There are games that suggest to your dog that he is the boss, and you want to avoid them. They include playing rough games, such as tug-of-war and wrestling. Play games that make him work for you; retrieving games are good.

Do *not* let him sleep in bed with you.

Do not allow your dog to engage you in a power struggle. If he argues with you, use his leash and collar to help him do what you want. Never, ever allow him to use his strength against you; it would be too easy for him to win.

Remember at all times that you are in fact the leader. Think like a leader; think assertive. Stand tall and act confident.

HAVE PEOPLE CAUSED THE PROBLEM?

As a dog obedience instructor, I watch how dog owners interact with their dogs every day and I marvel at how well dogs get along in our world. Unfortunately, we (the owners of dogs) are often the cause of behavior problems. And worse yet, the problems caused by the owners are the hardest to solve because it is harder to see problems within ourselves than it is to see the problems in our dogs.

With rescue dogs, it's even more challenging because the problem was possibly caused by a previous owner and carried on to his relationship with you.

Certain types of owners seem destined to have problems with their dogs. At the risk of over-generalizing, I would say they tend to fall into the following categories:

Demanding owners, who would prefer the dog to be a furry robot that follows each and every order exactly as given. Dogs, of course, will make mistakes. Dogs belonging to these owners will never measure up no matter how hard they try.

Over-emotional owners, who are quick to get excited or quick to react, often end up with dogs just like them. Unfortunately, during episodes of excitement, these dogs can get out of hand.

Over-protective owners, who prevent the dog from developing coping skills. By being "protected" from everything, the dog often becomes fearful; sometimes aggressively fearful.

Over-permissive owners, who don't set enough rules, or when they do set rules, do not enforce them. These owners are not the dog's leader and many problem behaviors can develop.

Shy, timid owners, whose dogs seem to have one of two types of personality. Many timid people get a large, extroverted dog who can portray their bolder self. The dog may become over-protective of his timid owner, sometimes dangerously so. Or the shy owner may get a dog just like himself and the two will go through life very quietly.

Mean, nasty owners, who overpower their dogs, making the dogs fearful or fearful-aggressive. Because aggression begets aggression in certain dogs, these owners often wind up with a dog as mean as they are.

Many owners of rescue dogs are over-emotional and/or over-protective, especially if they believe the dog was mistreated, abused or neglected in his first home. Unfortunately, the vast majority of dog owners do not know how to read or understand canine body language. When their new dog displays submission or confusion, they assume the dog is reacting to previous abuse. These people, trying very hard to be

Unfortunately, many rescue dogs have developed some problem behaviors. Consistent training can resolve many of these behavior problems.

good dog owners, then become overly emotional and over-protective. This, in turn, creates more problems for the dog.

IS YOUR DOG'S LIFE DULL?

Most of the dog breeds we know today were bred to do a job. Some are herding dogs, some are gun dogs, some are retrievers and so on. If your rescue dog is a pet, living in your house with you, his working instincts are now sitting idle. You know the old saying, "Idle hands are the devil's workshop." Idle paws are, too!

A bored dog is going to get into trouble. What he does to entertain himself may vary—some dogs bark, some dig and some chew. You need to figure out how to alleviate some of his boredom.

Have frequent training sessions and keep his obedience skills good; this challenges his mind.

Get involved in a dog sport or activity so that he has something new and different to occupy his mind and body.

Increase his exercise so that he's more likely to sleep when left alone.

If he gets into trouble when left alone, give him a toy before you leave—a rawhide, a biscuit or a small paper bag with treats in it. A Kong toy stuffed with peanut butter or one of the new food dispensing toys will occupy him for hours.

If you are gone for long periods during the day, hire a dog walker, a neighbor or the neighbor's teenage daughter to come over and spend some time with your dog while you're at work.

Is Your Dog's Food Right for Him?

A lot of dogs will thrive on just about any food. However, for some dogs, diets consisting of over 50 percent carbohydrates are known to cause a type of hyperactivity. These dogs usually act like they simply cannot hold still, but they often calm significantly once switched over to a good-quality food that is higher in meat protein and significantly lower in cereal grain carbohydrates. A food that has carbohydrates from sweet potatoes and other vegetables (rather than cereals) is usually better for sensitive dogs.

Many dogs are also very sensitive to some food colorings, preservatives or other additives. Other dogs have food allergies that present themselves in both physical and behavioral symptoms.

If you suspect a food-related problem, consider changing foods, particularly if you are feeding a food high in cereal grain carbohydrates or high in synthetic additives. Don't forget, too, to talk to your veterinarian.

Change Gradually

If you do switch your dog from one food to another, take your time. Add a little of the new food to the old and gradually—over two weeks—add more of the new food.

IS YOUR DOG A COUCH POTATO?

Lack of sufficient exercise is connected with many unwanted behaviors. A rescue dog who hasn't gotten enough exercise may be ready to bounce off the walls! A young, healthy dog needs to run, explore and use up his energy. If he doesn't get a chance to do so, he's likely to do it in the house. Or he's going to do something else to burn off calories and alleviate stress, such as pace, dig, bark or destroy things.

A dog who doesn't get enough exercise has other problems too, including health problems. Just as we are getting more sedentary, so are our dogs. Experts say that more people are overweight today than at any time during recorded history and veterinarians say the same thing about our dogs. An overweight dog is not happy, nor is he healthy. Regular aerobic exercise can help use up your dog's excess energy and can help keep his weight at a healthy level.

The amount of exercise needed will vary from dog to dog. A nice mile walk around the neighborhood would be enough for a tiny toy breed dog, but a five-mile jog would be better for a full-grown, healthy adult herding breed dog. Tailor your exercise to your individual dog.

CHANGING BAD BEHAVIORS

Changing problem behavior requires a commitment from you. You are going to have to be involved in the process, which may require you to make some changes. You may have to make some physical changes around the house or yard, or you may have to make some alterations in your daily schedule. If you make the effort, however, your chances of success are greatly increased. Most canine behavior problems can be modified, and if not cured, at least controlled.

Let's start at the beginning:

Make sure your rescue dog is healthy. Don't assume he is healthy; make an appointment with your veterinarian.

Make and keep a regular schedule for training. Fifteen minutes of sit, lie down, stay, heel and come—all on leash—will help keep his skills sharp and his mind attentive.

Use his training around the house and yard, and when out in public. Training is not just for training sessions!

Make sure your dog gets regular, vigorous exercise.

Make the time for play and have fun with your dog. Wasn't that one of the main reasons you got him?

Make sure your rescue dog gets enough vigorous exercise.

Prevent the problems from occurring when you can. Put away the trash cans, pick up the children's toys and put away the cushions for the lawn furniture.

Teach the dog an alternative behavior to the one you don't like. He can't jump on you if he learns to sit for petting. He can't dash out the front door if he has been taught to sit and wait at the door.

Set your rescue dog up to learn. When you can't closely supervise him and catch him in the act, arrange things so he makes a mistake when you're there to teach him the way you want him to behave.

SOME SOLUTIONS TO THE MOST COMMON PROBLEMS

Long ago I gave up on trying to find a magic wand that I could wave over a dog's head to cure his problem behaviors. Every wand I found seemed to be defective; it just didn't work! However, over the years I have found a few solutions that (with work!) help alleviate problem behaviors for a great number of dogs.

SEPARATION ANXIETY

Many newly adopted rescue dogs suffer from separation anxiety. Having lost one (or more) homes, these dogs don't want to be away from you for a moment and when left home alone, will often react by barking, crying or screaming. Others will act out destructively, chewing up furniture, shoes or anything else within reach. Some try to escape from their crate, the house or the fenced-in yard and don't seem to notice when they harm themselves in the process.

Separation anxiety can be very difficult to mitigate, but there are some new medications that can calm the dog's anxiety while you work on changing behaviors. Talk to your veterinarian about this type of treatment. Because this problem is so challenging, you'll also want to consult with your dog trainer or behaviorist about working specifically on it. In the meantime, make leave-takings and homecomings quiet and calm. Don't make a fuss as you come and go; just do so calmly and without emotion. When you leave, leave your dog in a safe place with a food-dispensing toy.

JUMPING ON PEOPLE

To stop your dog from jumping up on people, teach him to sit instead. This may seem very simple, but when the dog learns to sit for attention, including petting from you, he will sit in front of you quivering in anticipation of his reward, and will have no need to jump on you. If you consistently reward him for sitting, the jumping behavior will disappear.

LIMIT FREEDOM

Preventing problems from occurring may mean limiting your rescue dog's freedom. Don't let him have free run of the house, and supervise him closely. This is just as important now as it was when you were working on his housetraining skills.

You will also have to teach him to sit for other people. Use his leash and simply do not allow him to jump up. Have him sit first (before people greet him) and then when he tries to jump, use a snap and release correction as you tell him, "No jump!" Make him sit and don't permit others to pet him until he's sitting. Teaching your dog to sit instead of jumping up requires consistency in training. *Everyone* must make sure the dog sits; if someone does not apply the rule, the dog will continue to jump up.

BARKING

Dogs bark for a number of reasons. Protective dogs bark to warn you of trespassers—real or imagined. Social dogs bark to communicate with you and the world around them. Dogs bark at the kids playing out front, the birds flying overhead and the neighbor's dog barking down the block. Unfortunately, a barking dog is also a nuisance; sometimes a significant nuisance.

Start correcting barking in the house when you are close. Make up a squirt bottle with about one-eighth white vinegar and the rest water. (You want just enough vinegar so you can smell it but not enough to hurt your dog's eyes.) When someone comes to the door, for example, and your dog barks, walk quietly to the dog, tell him, "Quiet!" firmly but without yelling. Mist the vinegar water toward him. He will smell the vinegar, stop barking, back off and maybe even sneeze. When he stops barking, tell him, "Good boy to be quiet!"

You have stopped the behavior (with the squirt bottle) so that you can tell him what he did wrong, "Quiet!" and then when he was quiet, you praised him for being quiet. Very good dog training!

If you yell at your dog to stop barking (most people's first reaction), you're doing the same thing he's doing— making lots of noise at the front door. To your dog, you're barking too! So of course he isn't going to stop, he thinks you're the reinforcements!

DISTRACTIONS

A distraction also works for many "home alone" barkers. Give him a Buster Cube or Kong before you leave and he won't even know you've left!

The toys that dispense treats can distract a dog who is prone to problem behaviors when left alone.

Once your dog has learned what the word "quiet" means, start asking him to be quiet in other situations. Whenever he starts to bark inappropriately, tell him to be quiet and back up your command. Again, always praise him for being quiet when he stops.

If your dog barks when you're not home, you may have to set up a situation so you can catch him in the act. Go through all the motions of leaving—get dressed, pick up your purse, wallet or briefcase—get in the car and drive down the block. Park the car down the block and walk back with squirt bottle in hand. When your dog starts to bark, surprise him with a "Quiet!" and a squirt! If you set him up a few times, he will quickly learn that you have much more control than he thought!

I do *not* recommend most of the electronic anti-bark collars for rescue dogs. If you feel you have a serious barking problem and would like to try one of these collars, call a trainer or behaviorist for help first. These collars must be used correctly. Incorrect use could harm your dog.

There is, however, a new collar on the market that has worked very well for some rescue dogs. This collar, instead of administering a shock, responds to the barking by squirting out a burst of citronella spray. Working on the same principle as the vinegar squirt bottle, it offends the rescue dog's sense of smell, stopping the barking, usually in mid-bark!

BAD HABIT!

Destructive chewing is not just a bad habit; it can threaten your dog's life should he chew on the wrong thing. Make sure anything that is poisonous is locked up, away from your dog.

DESTRUCTIVE CHEWING

Unwanted chewing isn't a hard problem to solve if you carefully follow a few guidelines. Riker, my youngest dog, has never chewed up anything inappropriate. During his entire puppyhood, he never destroyed anything he shouldn't have! Before you ask, let me reassure you, no, he didn't spend his entire puppyhood in a crate, he lived in the house with us. However, I will share some of my secrets with you.

First, consistently correct the dog each and every time he puts his mouth on something he shouldn't. Follow up each and every correction by handing him one of his toys. You show him what's wrong, "No! That's mine," and take the wrong item away as you tell him, "Here, this is your toy. Good boy!" and hand him his toy.

Prevent unwanted chewing from occurring as much as you possibly can. That means never allowing your dog to have unsupervised access to stuff that can be destroyed.

Don't let him have free run of the house; close bedroom doors, put up baby gates and keep him close to you.

Never assume that your dog knows what he can chew and what he can't. He'll understand with time; that's why you're teaching him now.

Walk around the house, yard and garage with your dog and watch what he's interested in. What strikes his fancy? What does he want to get into? How can you prevent him from destroying those things? Be proactive and stop the behavior from happening before he actually does it!

DIGGING

Many dogs will dig a small hole (usually in a corner of the garden) to bury a favorite toy or bone and some will dig a shallow hole to use as a nest. These minor holes can usually be excused and ignored; but the dogs who want to dig under the fence or those who wish to tunnel to China can be a major problem.

Most digging occurs when the owner is not at home. Rarely does it happen when you're there to witness it, and that's too bad, because to correct it, you have to catch the dog in the act. Correcting him later, when you come home and discover it, does not work.

As with much of behavior correction, prevention is the key. When you're not home, don't let the dog have free access to the lawn and gardens. Build him a dog run where he can do anything he wants. Then, when you're at home, you can let him run around the backyard and when you see him start to dig (or sniff the gopher holes), you can interrupt and teach him, "Acckk! No dig!"

To show your rescue dog the place where he can dig, find a spot in the yard, perhaps behind the garage or in an out-of-the-way corner, where you can dig up the soil. Using a shovel, loosen the dirt really well. Take half a dozen dog biscuits and stick them in the dirt so they are only partially covered. Invite your dog to find the biscuits and to dig here. After he finds the biscuits, completely bury a few so he has to dig for them. It's not a bad idea to even help him dig them up at first. For the first few days, continue to bury something in this spot and invite him to find it. When he digs elsewhere, correct him and take him back to his spot; he'll learn where he may and may not dig.

MOUTHING AND BITING

It is very natural for your dog to use his mouth in play or to make you do (or stop doing) something—after all, he doesn't have any hands! However, biting cannot be allowed to happen for any reason. It only takes one bite for authorities to confiscate your dog and kill him. In many states today (due to so many horrible dog bite episodes), the state need show no aggressive intent to remove your dog. Legally, a bite is a bite regardless of the dog's intent. That means if your dog tries to "herd"

BIG TROUBLE!

If your dog bites someone, not only can your dog be killed but depending on where you live, you can also face a lawsuit from the victim, medical costs, criminal charges, a fine and possibly even jail time!

the neighbor's kids while they are running with your kids in your backyard, and nips one of the kids on the back of the leg, that nip is considered a bite. Your dog doesn't need to display any viciousness or vicious intent.

The Centers for Disease Control in Atlanta, Georgia, has declared a "dog bite epidemic," indicating that over one million dog bite cases are reported yearly. When you consider that these are only the bites requiring medical attention, the numbers of actual bites are probably twice to three times this number.

Every dog must learn that touching teeth to skin or clothing is *absolutely* forbidden. Be consistent. Don't allow your dog to nip you during play and then correct him for nipping in other situations.

Don't play games that teach him to use his strength against you, and don't allow anyone else to play this way with him. No tug-of-war and no wrestling.

Don't allow the dog to chase the children and don't allow him to "herd" the kids, nipping at their heels or clothing.

Teach the children to play quietly with the dog; running and screaming tend to get a dog excited and to provoke unwanted incidents.

Don't allow your dog to grab at his leash, chew on it, mouth it or put it in his mouth and pull against it.

There are several ways to correct mouthing and biting. No one of these corrections is better or worse than the others; some are more useful in certain situations. Use the squirt bottle (one-eighth vinegar to seven-eighths water) for those instances where the dog is nipping at your legs, heels or clothes. Have the squirt bottle in hand in those situations (or times) when you know he is apt to do it. When he nips at your heels, squirt him as you tell him, "No bite!" When he backs off, praise him quietly, "Good boy."

TEMPER TANTRUM

A temper tantrum is when your young rescue dog (usually an adolescent) protests something you're doing to him by throwing himself around, crying, growling or screaming and often by trying to bite you. A temper tantrum is bad behavior on his part. Do not give in. If he wants you to stop brushing him, for example, when the tantrum is over, continue brushing him! If you stop, he learns that the temper tantrum works!

If you have your hands on your dog, perhaps when hooking up his leash, playing with him or petting him, and he tries to mouth or bite you, correct him right away without hesitation. With one hand, grab his buckle collar or the scruff of his neck (as a handle) and with the other hand simply close his mouth. Tell him firmly, "No bite!" Do not let go of his muzzle until he takes a deep sigh and relaxes. If you let go and he continues to try to mouth or bite you, close his mouth again, correct him again and wait him out. You are the leader and the boss.

When you're teaching your dog, don't lose your temper. Aggression begets aggression and if you get angry and lose your temper, your dog may very well retaliate. If you lose your temper often; his behavior may mirror your own, becoming more aggressive in response to you. When you correct biting and mouthing, correct him fairly and firmly (just as you did any other behavior) without losing your cool.

Make sure you praise your dog when he doesn't put his mouth on you, especially in situations where he might have done so prior to your training. Remember, corrections tell the dog when he made a mistake but praise shows him what to continue doing!

SUGGESTIONS FOR OTHER PROBLEMS

Over time, there might be a few other things come up that you don't want to live with, and if that happens, don't panic. Many behaviors can be changed or prevented with a minimum of fuss.

For example, to alleviate digging under the fence, bury some rocks in the holes he digs. Then try to understand why he is digging under the fence. Make sure he's getting enough exercise, playtime and attention from you.

To deal with chasing cars, kids on in-line skates, bikes and skateboards, keep him on leash and when he tries to chase, correct him with the leash and have him sit. Enforce the sit and sit/stay. If he can't sit still, turn around, walk the other direction and if he doesn't walk with you, let the leash correct him. Praise him when he does walk with you.

Some dogs get a thing about barking in the car. Ideally, have your dog ride in a crate in the car. This is much safer for him than riding on the seat. However, if he is big and a crate doesn't fit in your car, use our magic training tool, the squirt bottle. As you're driving, when your dog barks, just grab the squirt bottle and spray a sweeping mist in the direction of your dog as you tell him, "Quiet!" Don't even turn to look at him, which could cause you to run off the road or into the back of another car.

A BRIEF REVIEW OF THE PROCESS

As I mentioned earlier in this chapter, more dogs are given up by their owners due to problem behaviors than for any other single reason. This is tragic when so many problems can be stopped or controlled.

When your dog acts in a way that you dislike, follow these steps:

1. Make sure you are your dog's leader.

2. Examine why your dog is doing this. Look at it from his point of view; not yours! Is he getting enough exercise? Are you spending enough time with him? Does he have a health problem that might be causing him to act this way? Are neighborhood kids teasing him outside the fence?

3. How can you teach him? Set him up so that the problem will happen while you're at home and able to correct him. Make sure you praise him if he decides not to do it!

4. Can you prevent the problem from occurring? Will a dog run help? Or a different use of his crate? Does your dog need more supervision?

5. Practice his obedience commands regularly and use them around the house and yard. Incorporate them into your daily routine.

With your energy and commitment, it's likely that you'll be able to satisfactorily resolve the problem.

CHAPTER 12

AGGRESSION

The word "aggression" has become a catchall term for a variety of behaviors that are very natural to dogs. When a mother dog growls, snaps and lunges at someone moving toward her puppies, that is innate, protective, aggressive behavior. In the world of dogs and other canines, she is supposed to protect her offspring. When a dog is barking at the front door as a stranger approaches, that, too, is correct conduct in the world of dogs. That dog is protecting her territory against a stranger, a trespasser and a potential threat. In human society, many natural canine behaviors must be tempered and controlled (such as leg lifting to mark territory in the house!), and aggression is one of them.

Aggression is a very complex behavioral issue, and many books have been written on the subject. Obviously, I cannot explain the subject fully in these pages. However, it is important to at least explore the topic so that you can understand whether your rescue dog has a problem and to give you some guidance.

AGGRESSION IS NATURAL

Many breeds of dogs in existence today were bred to be protective of their property or people. Rottweilers were bred to be multi-purpose dogs, one of which was to serve as a guard dog. Although Rotties today are wonderful family dogs, they still have strong territorial defensive traits. Doberman Pinschers, Akitas and Boxers are very protective, and dogs of many herding breeds, including German Shepherds and Australian Shepherds, are also very territorial and protective. A protective dog will bark, growl and lunge toward a threat. This is very natural aggression.

A dog with protective instincts will show aggression to protect her home, her land, her owner's possessions, her owner's vehicle, her owner's children, her owner's livestock and of course, her owner. A dog with a stable, balanced temperament and good training can use aggression appropriately with no problems. The only risk would be to trespassers or thieves.

However, dogs with a less than stellar temperament or a dog with no or poor training could be a severe liability. A dog who is too aggressive could use that aggression in inappropriate situations, perhaps biting before barking or showing aggression to those who are not a threat. The ultimate in inappropriate aggression occurs when a dog attacks a child, or bites her owner or her owner's family.

WHAT IS A DOG BITE?

When a dog attacks someone, grabbing and tearing the skin, causing bleeding and obvious physical harm, we know we can call that a dog bite. But what if the bite is less harmful? What if the dog puts her mouth on someone's arm but doesn't break the skin? Is that a bite, too? Or how about a herding dog pinching the back of a person's calf?

In many cities, counties and states today, a dog bite is defined as the dog's mouth or teeth touching skin or clothing. Aggressive or vicious intent (which used to be a part of the dog bite definition) is often no longer a necessary element of the offense. In other words, if your dog grabs your neighbor's son by the jeans and pinches his leg, even if no blood is drawn, it can still be considered a bite.

The change in definition is a legislative response to some dog bite incidences in which people (including children) were horribly mauled or killed. Media attention to these events sent people clamoring for action. New laws, and more punitive laws, were one result.

Unfortunately, much of the legislation concerning dog bites have an emotional, rather than a strongly reasoned, foundation. For example, a law outlawing ownership of a certain breed is often the first reaction to a bad bite incident. Although some breeds can deliver a worse bite than others (due to size, jaw shape and power, overall strength and the like) that does not mean that any one breed is more likely to bite than another. Legislation making it illegal to own a particular breed on this basis is ill informed, at best.

If a dog has teeth, she can bite. Some old dogs without teeth still try to bite! All dogs are capable of biting, however, not all dogs will bite people.

Although some breeds have a reputation for being aggressive, this is an unfair label. Individual dogs can be aggressive, but whole breeds are not. This German Shepherd dog is a certified therapy dog.

DEFINING PROBLEM AGGRESSION

Most rescue dog organizations screen the dogs in their programs for aggression. Dogs showing undue aggression and those who have already bitten people are rarely accepted into a rescue program. The Aussie Rescue & Placement Helpline and the Bulldog Club of America Rescue Program, as do many other programs, expressly state that aggressive dogs will not be accepted.

However, that doesn't mean that a rescue dog will never be aggressive. Either aggressive behavior may surface later, as the dog grows older and perhaps more confident, or it may surface during the dog's transfer to a new home. Remember that some rescue groups serve only as referral organizations; putting relinquishing owners in touch with potential adopters. In these situations, an experienced rescue volunteer may never even see the dog and a dog's aggressive tendencies, or potential for aggression, would be unknown.

Moreover, identifying an aggressive dog, especially your own, can be difficult. Dog owners don't want to admit their dog is aggressive. After all, she's their dog; their new best friend, and no one wants to admit their best friend has a potentially dangerous problem. But with aggression, it is much more important to address the reality than to deny it.

DISPLAYS OF AGGRESSION

If your dog growls while you're playing with her, that's not necessarily aggression. Many dogs "talk" while playing—that's expected and very natural. Similarly, if your dog growls while "talking" to you, for example, when asking you for a treat; that, too, is natural and is not necessarily aggressive. If, while you are interacting with your dog, her body language is relaxed, her ears are soft and relaxed and her tail is wagging happily while talking to you, she is not acting aggressively.

However, you may have a problem if: Your dog growls and protects her toy while you're playing and will not allow you to touch the toy. Your dog growls while trying to make you do something and will not

SOME COMMON EXCUSES

Dog owners never expect their own dog to bite them and tend to make excuses to cover up their dog's bad behavior. Here are some excuses I have heard in my dog training classes:

I disturbed her while she was eating.

My dog doesn't like kids.

My dog was too excited to think.

My dog doesn't like my husband to kiss me.

My dog is angry at me because _____ (fill in the blank).

My dog doesn't like _____ (fill in the blank).

My dog was guarding _____ (fill in the blank).

None of the above is a real reason for aggressive behavior.

accept no for an answer. Your dog growls at you while you are brushing her and snaps at your hands, with ears back and body stiff. Your dog guards her food, growling and snapping. Your dog appears very fearful and snaps often.

You do have a problem if: Your dog stares at you while on tiptoes, making direct eye contact, with her hackles up. Your dog has made you feel uncomfortable or afraid.

FEARFUL AGGRESSION

There are many causes and types of aggression. There is territorial aggression and dominance-related aggression. Most dogs protecting their territory, property or themselves will growl, bark and even lunge but often are not eager to bite. For most dogs a bite is the last resort. A fearful dog, however, may be reacting to that emotion and may feel she has no choice. A fearful dog may bite quickly, readily and hard.

An aggressive dog is usually bold. She will stand tall and lean forward. Her ears are forward, her head is up and pushing forward and while on her toes, she will lean her body forward. The aggressive dog is usually quite straightforward, too, with her emotions. If she is being protective or is angry, she is showing those emotions. There is no mistaking her intent and in this respect, she is usually very predictable.

The fearful dog, however, might display conflicting body language. She may move toward you, looking aggressive and intent, yet her tail may be tucked under her back legs, showing her fear and ambivalence. Her head may be up, or she may carry it low, depending upon her level of confidence or lack of it. The fearful dog is much more apt to bite than the purely aggressive dog, and for less reason. In fact, the reasons that many fearful dogs bite often don't seem to make any sense. She may be fine while you pet her head but may bite you when you pet her chest. Or she may bite when you walk too quickly past her bed. Fearful dogs are often unpredictable and difficult to control.

PREVENTION AND CORRECTION

If your rescue dog was raised by an informed and responsible dog owner, you may not have any aggression problems. All you will need to do is continue what your dog's first owner began. However, if your dog was not quite this lucky, you will have to begin fresh and hope that your dog's history can be left behind.

As I have mentioned several times in previous chapters, your dog needs a leader. If you adopted a dog because you wanted a dog to be your best friend, that's fine, you can still be your dog's leader. In fact, if you don't provide the guidance of a leader, your dog will not be your best friend! Without a leader, your dog is adrift and must make up her own rules, and those rules will not be the ones you want. Good leaders are kind and caring, yet firm and fair; and their rules are clear and enforced all the time. Good leaders set a good example, follow their own rules and always win the games. Leaders stand tall and carry themselves with confidence.

Training will help you establish yourself as your dog's leader if you train kindly and humanely, yet firmly. Be clear about what you expect from your dog and communicate well so there is little confusion. Through training, your dog will understand what is expected of her, and she will also get a sense of security in her relationship with you. As I've said earlier, use your training around the house, on your walks and out in public.

If you are training your rescue dog with the help of a professional trainer, they will help you perfect your human-canine communication skills. A mastery of these skills is extremely important, as miscommunications result in many behavior problems. When dealing with a potentially aggressive dog, good communication is vital. For example, if your dog barks at your neighbor who has walked past to go to the mailbox, what would you do? If you pet your dog, hold her close and tell her, "That's okay, Bubbles, be a good girl," what have you really told your

THE BEAUTY OF THE "DOWN/STAY" COMMAND

The "down/stay" command teaches the dog to lie down and stay in one place. It also teaches her to hold that position for as long as you want her to do so. On the surface, this may seem like a simple obedience command, but it's much more than that. By teaching your dog that you can have her do this, that she is required to cooperate, and that you can ask her to cooperate for a period of time, you are again establishing yourself as her leader. Have your dog lie down and stay while you're eating, or when guests come over or have her do it when she's ignoring your household rules.

AGGRESSION BEGETS AGGRESSION

When correcting mouthing, biting or any other aggressive behavior, be aware that aggression begets aggression. If you are aggressive toward your dog, you risk exacerbating the problem. Therefore when stopping, correcting or redirecting aggressive (or potentially aggressive) behavior, be calm and firm. Do not get angry or act aggressively yourself.

dog? Have you told her that barking at your neighbor was inappropriate? No, you haven't. You told Bubbles with your soft words and petting that her barking at your neighbor was the right thing to do. You praised and rewarded her for barking at your neighbor. What you should have done instead was say in a sharp firm voice, "Acck! That's enough! Quiet!" If that did not stop her barking, a repeat of the command in a firmer voice backed up with a snap and release of the leash would have been appropriate.

I must repeat another point I've made previously. You must be willing to limit your rescue dog's freedom. She should not have free run of the house until she has earned it by showing consistent good behavior and until she has demonstrated the mental maturity to handle the responsibility of the freedom. Many dogs are three, four or even five years old before given free, unsupervised run of the house. Some dogs are never able to handle the responsibility.

If you feel that your rescue dog may have some aggressive tendencies, discontinue all types of play and games that have her play rough against you. Don't wrestle with her, don't play tug-of-war and stop all physical rough play. You don't want your dog to think that using her strength against you is acceptable in any situation.

Don't let your dog bite your hands for any reason, even in play. Don't allow her to bite or pull on your clothes or to nip your heels. Play-biting can easily turn into more forceful biting. You can stop the mouthing and biting by discontinuing games before she becomes overstimulated (and more likely to bite) or by changing the games you play. If she tries to mouth or bite when you are petting her, or grooming her, or when you put her collar on, simply tell her, "Acck! No bite!" and gently close her muzzle with one hand while you hold her collar with the other (so she can't pull her head away).

OVER-CODDLING

One of the best ways to make a young rescue dog aggressive is to over-coddle her. An older rescue dog may be able to get through this without too much damage, but a young dog may be ruined by it. Over-coddling, unfortunately, is very common behavior by people who have adopted a rescue dog. Because they believe that they are "saving" a dog who may have been neglected, ignored, mistreated or abused, these owners feel the dog should be treated like royalty to "make up" for past abuses. The reality is that not as many rescue dogs have been abused as adopters seem to feel, and over-coddling any dog (regardless of her history) is not the answer.

Over-coddling is sheltering the dog from reality. An over-coddled rescue dog is never disturbed, or alone, or corrected. Nothing that the adoptive owners feel is negative ever happens to these dogs. By being so over-protected, these rescue dogs never learn any social manners or household rules. Obedience commands are performed only if the dog wishes to do them, and so the owner is never the dog's leader.

Over-coddling creates a dog who has no leader, no guidance, no rules in the house or outside and is adrift in a human world. She will often act out destructively in the house, often lose housetraining skills and very often react aggressively toward people. Dogs can and should be well loved; but they must be well loved within boundaries by a respected owner who is also in charge.

POTENTIAL SOLUTIONS TO SOME COMMON PROBLEMS

Most rescue dogs are spayed and neutered, but if your dog is not, have this procedure performed right away. Spaying a female dog can affect aggressive tendencies, although not as significantly as neutering males does. Intact (un-neutered) males can be very macho, and those with aggressive tendencies are more prone to following through with a bite. A good pet has no need for these hormones. Get your dog spayed or neutered.

Use a leash in the house as much as you need to. If your dog likes to steal your stuff and then play "keep away," (all the while growling while guarding the items), don't try to grab her. Instead, use the leash! As she goes running past you with your shoe in her mouth, don't chase her. Instead, step on the leash as she goes past. Stop her abruptly and while she is still startled about her game being interrupted, take away your shoe. Then have her do a long (at least five minutes) down/stay.

The leash is also good for dogs who plop themselves on the bed or sofa and growl when you try to make them move. If the dog is off leash, making her move might result in a snap or bite. However, if the dog is on leash, you can use the leash to get the dog off the bed or sofa while issuing a stern verbal correction, "Hey! Get off the bed! Don't growl at me! Quiet!" The leash is also a great tool for extricating dogs who hide under the bed and refuse to come out.

If you are in the habit of holding the leash tightly, keeping pressure on your dog's neck, you may be creating a problem. Many dogs feel braver on leash, and when the leash is tight, they show more aggression. Perhaps they feel the connection to you and know you are there as backup. If you have noticed this tendency in your dog, try to keep the leash loose in those situations where your dog shows aggression. That means you may have to allow yourself and your dog more room so that she can move on a loose leash. You may have to also emphasize her training, especially the "no pulling on the leash" rule so that she doesn't continually tighten the leash.

Many dog owners are under the misconception that because dogs are social animals, they should all get along. They don't! Wolves are social animals, too, but will often fight wolves from another pack, particularly if the other pack trespasses into their territory. Dogs will usually get along with other dogs they know, such as your mom's dog or the dog next door. But strange dogs are often considered a potential threat and to a protective dog, that is war! Many dogs simply have no desire (or need) to get along with strange dogs. You need to know your dog, be aware of her personality and protect her (even from herself). If she doesn't like other dogs, don't force her into situations where she'll do something you don't want her to do—such as pick a fight with other dogs.

USING THE LEASH IN THE HOUSE

Use the leash wisely. When your dog is in the house with you, close to you, and you can supervise her, let her drag the leash. If you cannot supervise, take the leash off. You don't want her to get the leash tangled and choke or hang herself.

....

DOG PARKS

Off-leash dog parks are becoming increasingly popular as more and more towns do not permit dogs to run free. Dog parks can be wonderful for dogs who get along with other dogs. However, dog parks can be a recipe for disaster for dogs who have no desire to play with strange dogs. Getting along with strangers is not natural for many dog breeds. So know your own dog and don't force the issue!

....

Does your dog go nuts when the mail carrier delivers your mail? Or when the overnight courier comes to your door? That's because your dog barks when they show up and then she chases them away. She wins every single time! To control this, plan ahead and have your dog on leash before they are due to arrive. When she barks, praise her for barking and then tell her to stop. If she continues, correct her. Praise her when she's quiet.

SOME COMMON (BUT POOR) ADVICE

All dog trainers, as I mentioned before, have their own techniques or methods for training dogs, and that includes how to work with aggressive dogs. However, there are some techniques offered that may actually make aggressive dogs worse.

One way to reinforce aggression is to use it. Do not hit or slap the dog with your hands, with a rolled-up newspaper, a stick, a yardstick or anything else. Don't kick the dog. Aggression begets aggression. If you are aggressive with your dog, your dog will react with aggression. Your dog may feel she has to fight back or protect herself. If she is fearful, she may not even think, she may simply bite when you attack her. And that's what hitting or kicking is, an attack.

Do not attack your dog in other ways under the name of punishment or correction. Do not pinch or twist her ears, grab her tongue, stab a fingernail into the roof of her mouth or bite her. These are not punishments or corrections; they are physical attacks on the dog.

Do not hang the dog by her collar until she passes out. Do not shake her until her head rattles. Do not pick her up and throw her to the ground and sit on her—some trainers encourage you to do this, calling the action an "alpha rollover" or "dominance down."

Instead, use training techniques that are calm and fair yet firm. If you suspect that your techniques might be too rough, you're probably right.

WHEN YOU NEED HELP

If your dog is simply barking at people approaching your house and has made no effort to take the barking any further, you can probably train your dog yourself. However, if at any point you begin to feel uncomfortable, or worse yet, you feel that your dog could possibly bite you or someone else, call for help.

Call the rescue group from which you adopted your dog first. The group needs to be apprised of the situation. A volunteer might also be able to refer you to a trainer or behaviorist experienced in working with aggressive dogs. If someone can't refer you, call your obedience trainer and ask whether they can help you or if they can give you a referral.

Don't wait until your dog has bitten someone to seek out help. Aggression is much easier to resolve in its early stages than it is when it's become an ingrained pattern. When aggression has become a habit, and when the dog has already bitten, it can be very difficult to control.

If your dog is showing considerable aggression and you have discussed it with the rescue group volunteers and a professional trainer has been no help, you may have to consider that the problem is not solvable. The rescue group members or trainer may recommend euthanasia. In situations where the dog is uncontrollable and is a real danger to other dogs and people, euthanasia is often the only option. This is a very difficult decision to make and it should be. For guidance, don't hesitate to consult with the professionals you are working with and whose opinion you trust. Ultimately, however, the decision must be yours.

DOGFIGHT!

If your dog is involved in a dogfight, don't try to reach in and separate the dogs by grabbing their collars. You will get bitten and could get bitten badly. Instead, have the other dog's owner grab their dog's back legs as you grab the back legs of your dog. At the same time, lift and separate. Don't let either dog down until the dogs have stopped growling and snarling. Then let them down at the same time as you each grab your own dog's collar. Then turn them away from each other.

CHAPTER 13

• •

WHEN IT JUST ISN'T WORKING

In a perfect world, every dog would stay in his original loving, caring, responsible home for his lifetime. In a perfect rescue world, every adoption would work out wonderfully. Unfortunately, we don't live in a perfect world, and purebred rescue dog adoptions don't always have the outcome we hope for.

If you are getting the feeling that things are not working out the way you wanted them to, take a look at the situation. Is there anything you can do to improve it? Is the problem with the dog or with you? Talk to a trainer; talk to your veterinarian; and talk to the rescue group volunteers. If you find that you and your dog aren't developing a good relationship, give the dog back to the rescue group. Don't keep a dog who isn't working out just because you don't want to admit failure; that isn't fair to you or your dog.

LISTEN TO YOUR INTUITION

Many dog owners who have given up a dog say they knew when it wasn't working. Once in a while there was a concrete incident (such as a dog bite), but usually it was just a feeling, a gut feeling or intuition, that the relationship was not going to jell. Sometimes this is the result of a clash of personalities, perhaps your dog is an active extrovert while you are much quieter, and the dog's personality is driving you nuts. Sometimes it's the result of the dog being unable to bond with people, due perhaps to the dog's personality or due to bad experiences in the dog's past.

The dog may not be working out simply because you chose the wrong dog. Not every dog is right for every owner. For example, I love dogs; they are my professions (multiple—dog writer and dog trainer), and my husband and I share our home with three dogs. However, I really do dislike one of my mother's dogs. He is a nice dog, and my mom loves him dearly. As horrible as it sounds, I just don't like him. If I had adopted him, he would be going back to the rescue group. Personalities can clash. Rescue group volunteers hope that this type of inability to connect can be discovered during the introduction process prior to adoption, but sometimes the wrong dog is adopted by the wrong owner.

Some signs there is a problem:

- You don't feel a bond with the dog.
- You are constantly angry when around the dog.
- Your anger has escalated on occasion and you feel that you could harm the dog.
- The dog doesn't appear to care about you.
- You feel uncomfortable with the dog; even have a feeling of unease.
- You are afraid of the dog.
- The dog is growling or snapping at you or family members.
- The dog doesn't like your children and is growling, snapping or lunging.
- The dog has bitten someone since you adopted him.
- The dog has problem behaviors that have not gotten better with training or behavioral help and are getting more difficult to live with.

Whatever the reason, it is much better to admit there is a problem and change the situation than to continue on with a dysfunctional relationship. A bad relationship will cause both you and your dog pain.

CONSULT WITH PROFESSIONALS

Can you put a finger on exactly what is wrong with the situation? Is it behavioral? Can you talk to a trainer or behaviorist? If you can, discuss your feelings. They may have some ideas or suggestions that could work on the problem and potentially mend the relationship.

Is the problem related to the dog's breed, perhaps? Talk to the rescue group volunteers and sound them out. They have met with many people trying to build relationships with rescue dogs, and they may have some suggestions. Some dog breeds, for example, take longer than others to bond with their new owners. Perhaps you are expecting too much too soon and should just be a little more patient.

Talk to your veterinarian, too. A complete physical for the dog may be in order. Perhaps a thyroid problem is affecting the dog's behavior, or perhaps medication the dog is on is connected with one or more unwanted behaviors.

RE-DECIDING THE ADOPTION

If you have consulted with the professionals you know and cannot arrive at a satisfactory solution, contact the rescue group about giving back the dog. Group members have had this experience in the past and although they will want to know that you have done everything you can to make it work, they will take back the dog.

Don't take your dog to the local shelter and turn him in there. And of course you would never take the dog out in the country and abandon him! Always contact the rescue group from which you adopted him. Not only is this action a requirement of your adoption contract, but the rescue group can best manage the dog and his situation. They already know him and are experts in his breed.

Be honest with the volunteers and explain exactly what the problems were. They are going to want to decide whether this dog is adoptable and should be given a chance at another home or whether the dog is unadoptable and perhaps should be euthanized.

The rescue group has procedures for taking in dogs, and sometimes it may take a few days or even a few weeks for the transfer to occur. Be patient; remember, they may be managing the care of quite a few other dogs who also need homes. Your dog may need to wait until a kennel or foster home is available.

When you turn in your dog, bring his adoption paperwork, his health records (including vaccinations) and his favorite toys. Be calm and collected when you drop him off; no tears right now. An emotional farewell would simply make the event more difficult for the dog. Wait until the dog is taken away from you and then have a good cry.

STAND FIRM

If you know in your heart that you can't do anything more to resolve a bad situation with your rescue dog and then decide the dog needs to go back to rescue, fine. The decision is made. When you contact the rescue group, expect that one or two of the volunteers may try to talk you into keeping the dog. Sadly, some individuals have been known to use guilt as a bargaining tool: "If you don't keep him, we'll have to euthanize him." Don't change your mind under pressure. Living with a dog who is not right for you is bad for you, your family and for the dog. He knows he isn't loved!

SHOULD YOU HAVE A DOG?

Now comes the hardest part; should you get another dog? Was the problem with your dog or was the problem with you? Not everyone is a good dog owner, and not everyone should be one. Sometimes people have unrealistic expectations of what living with a dog is really like. Some people simply cannot stand the fuss and muss of living with a dog.

Once the dog is out of your household, take some time and look at yourself. What was it that didn't work? What was making you feel uncomfortable or was driving you crazy? Be as honest as you can with yourself, and if you can listen to others without feeling criticized, get the thoughts of another family member, your friends or the trainer you were working with. If you come to learn that your life isn't going to mesh well with that of a dog, so be it. There are lots of other ways to help animals in need, and ways to find companionship.

CHAPTER 14

DO YOU WANT TO
DO RESCUE WORK?

Rescue program volunteers get involved with rescue work for all sorts of reasons. Some like the fact that they are saving dogs' lives. Others care about the pet overpopulation problem and want to work toward that end. Many are born teachers and like to teach people about dogs. Some people like the challenge of fund-raising and have combined that with a love of dogs. Some volunteers want to help their chosen breed. The purebred dog rescue movement has a need for people from all walks of life with many different talents and skills.

CONTACT A RESCUE GROUP

If you are already familiar with a local group (perhaps the one from which you adopted your dog), give them a call. If you don't know of a local group or would prefer to work with a different group or breed, get in touch with your local humane society. It might maintain a list of local groups. See Chapter 4 for a discussion of various ways to find a rescue group.

When you have found a group, contact them and ask them what their needs are. Tell them what you might be able to do and where your skills lie. Don't call and tell them you would like to run the group or inform them of all the ways you can make their organization better. At this point, it is best to save your leadership skills for use with your dog. However, if you call and offer to help in a variety of ways, they will probably welcome you with open arms.

RESCUE GROUP JOBS

As with all volunteer organizations, there are always jobs that need doing. There is something for everyone no matter how much or how little time you can donate or what your skills are.

FOSTER HOMES

Most rescue groups maintain a network of foster homes where dogs awaiting adoption can be cared for until a new home is found. In a foster home a dog can be evaluated over a period of time. How is she with kids? Or with cats? Is she housetrained? Is she trustworthy in the house? Is she afraid of loud noises? Has she had any obedience training? The answers to these and other questions will allow the rescue group to better evaluate the individual dog and then place her in the right home. The adoptive owners will benefit, too, because they will know more about their dog.

Foster families take in dogs who need help and care for them until an adoptive home is found.

Foster homes are always in short supply. Kim Galloway, the AKC National Rescue Coordinator for American Eskimo rescue, said, "The biggest problem I have (with rescue) is the sheer number of dogs needing homes. I know I can't save them all but I have to try, and foster homes are slim to none." Unfortunately, foster care volunteers often offer to take in a dog, but then fall in love with her and adopt her. Although this is wonderful for the dog, the foster home may then be unable to take in another dog to foster. A new foster home is then needed to replace this one.

The requirements for foster home care vary from organization to organization, but most mandate that the dog be allowed to live in the house so she can be observed. The yard must be securely fenced, and a dog run is not a bad idea. You will need to have an appropriate-sized crate for the breed you are fostering. Your own dog must be safe and trustworthy with strange dogs. Extra dog equipment (leashes, bowls and so forth) is always helpful.

Some groups have other requirements. Some prefer that one person in the household stay home all day. Others want to know how many hours per day the dog will be alone. Group volunteers will also inquire about the dog's progress at regular intervals.

Many rescue groups ask that the dog begin learning basic obedience and household rules while in the foster home. Obviously, house-training must also be emphasized.

Fostering a dog can be difficult. You will be bringing home a dog you don't know, one who you may not necessarily choose to live with, and you will be keeping her for a period of time. You'll get to know her, probably grow to love her, and then at some time you will have to give her up. That's hard. The reward is, though, that you have given her a chance at a new life, and you have put her on the path to success in her new home.

ADMINISTRATIVE WORK

Volunteers are always, always, needed to return telephone calls and e-mails. These unglamorous tasks are very time-consuming but very necessary for the programs to succeed. When several people can share the work, it's much easier. If you have good interpersonal skills, enjoy talking on the phone and have a lot of patience, volunteer to help with this chore.

Today almost all rescue groups maintain a web site. Along with e-mail, the Internet has become a valuable tool for rescue. Many groups post their adoption policies on their web site as well as breed information. Most also have their adoption application available there, too. Potential adopters can fill it out and e-mail it in, or print it off and snail-mail it. Some web sites even post photos and descriptions of dogs available for adoption. If you have web site skills, let the rescue group know. Even if they already have a web site and a web site master, they may be able to use your skills.

HAVE VEHICLE, WILL TRAVEL

Transporting dogs is a task for which rescue volunteers are always in short supply. Dogs need to be picked up from relinquishing owners, taken to foster homes, picked up from foster homes, and so forth. Dogs will always need to be taken to the veterinarian's office and to the groomer. A roomy vehicle that can hold a crate or two (or three!) and a willing driver are always welcome!

Sometimes drivers are needed for long-distance runs. Occasionally relinquishing owners will need to have their dogs picked up and driven to foster homes or adoptive locations many miles away. Some dogs have been driven from one coast to another. In situations like this, most rescue groups ask for drivers to drive a section of the route where they live. For example, a driver living in New York may pick up the dog and drive her to Maryland, where another driver will take the dog and drive her to South Carolina, where another driver will take over. With coordination, dogs can be transported long distances.

PROFESSIONAL ASSISTANCE

Rescue groups are always in need of people with various professional skills. Records must be kept for both the dogs and the organization's activities. Taxes must be filed or reports generated. Financial records must be kept. There is always paperwork to be done.

Groups can also benefit from the time of professional groomers, because many rescue dogs come in needing baths, ear cleaning, nail trimming and grooming. Trainers and behaviorists can assist in evaluating dogs and guiding foster owners in training foster dogs. Trainers can also guide adoptive owners through the process of training their new dog. Because legal services are often expensive, rescue groups are always appreciative of low-cost or donated legal guidance. Veterinary care can also be expensive for rescue groups so when local veterinarians can donate their time to a group, it will help tremendously.

If you like to raise money, any rescue group will welcome your skills. Fund-raising is invariably a necessary, ongoing process for breed rescue organizations. If you know how to apply for grants, can send out fund-raising letters or even organize a car wash, volunteer your services.

OTHER SKILLS

If you have strong interpersonal abilities, rescue groups could use those skills, too. Volunteers must recruit new foster homes and new adoptive homes, and they must interview potential adopters. Someone must inspect homes and fences, discuss the adoption process and once in a while decline an application for adoption. Someone also needs to follow up after an adoption, making sure the relationship is working.

If you are a writer, have good computer skills and/or graphics arts knowledge, volunteer to help with the group's newsletter. If you take good photographs, volunteer to take photos of dogs available for adoption or those in their new homes. "Before-and-after" photos are often posted on the organization's web site.

Regardless of your inclinations, talents or skills, a rescue group can use your help. So call or e-mail and offer some time and energy.

THE DEMANDS OF RESCUE WORK

Be aware that rescue work can be tough. It can be dirty; cleaning up neglected, filthy dogs, and it can be emotionally draining. If you love dogs, it's hard to see dogs who have been treated poorly or are unloved. Kim Galloway said, "I do rescue because it breaks my heart to see so many loving healthy dogs tossed aside with no place to go. I can't turn my back on them as it is no fault of their own, but that of uncaring and irresponsible people!"

When doing rescue work, a positive attitude is essential. Sarah Filipak, the president of Pound Rescue of Athens, Ohio, said, "I do rescue work because it makes me feel good. I love dogs, love rescuing them and rehabilitating them. I love people and enjoy matching dogs with their new owners."

A positive attitude can help overcome the many frustrations. Rescuers who have come to the aid of injured, abused, neglected and sick dogs can easily become overwhelmed with anger. It is also impossible for any one person or rescue group to save every dog needing help. It is also very hard to make that decision not to save a dog; especially when you know your decision may result in a dog's death.

However, when you can save a dog's life, all your work, time and efforts are rewarded. When that dog is placed in a new home, you will feel such a sense of satisfaction and relief. Later, when you check up on that dog and find that she is now a loved, well-behaved member of the family, don't be surprised if you cry with happiness.

● ●

INTERNET RESOURCES FOR PUREBRED DOG RESCUE

The Internet has become a wonderful tool for rescue dog groups as well as dog owners. Through search engines, individuals can locate rescue groups all over the world as well in as the United States. In addition to information about dogs, dog training and health care, dog owners can learn about dog activities and sports.

One word of warning, however. Anyone can post anything to the Internet. Just because it's posted there doesn't mean it is true or that the person posting it is an authority. Verify credentials and double-check information before accepting it as valid.

Internet addresses can and do change rapidly. The following sites were active at the time of this writing.

PUREBRED DOG RESCUE GROUPS

The American Kennel Club maintains a list of national rescue coordinators for each national breed club. This list is published each November in the *AKC Gazette,* or you can find it at the AKC's web site, www.akc.org.

You can also find local or regional breed rescue groups by searching from a search engine (such as Google at www.google.com). For example, when I searched for "Australian Shepherd + rescue + San Diego" I came up with quite a few web sites that had information about San Diego rescue groups as well as quite a bit of general information about Aussies in that area.

CANINE CARE AND HEALTH

www.altvetmed.com: This is the main page for links to alternative veterinary medicine.

www.animalcare.ca: This is the official site for the veterinary profession in Canada, and offers a good deal of information about canine care.

www.avma.org: The American Veterinary Medical Association site offers information for veterinarians as well as for the dog-owning public.

www.canidae.com: The makers of Canidae dog foods offer information about their foods.

www.doctordog.com: A great resource for browsing, for researching or for emergency advice.

www.healthypet.com: The American Animal Hospital Association offers pet care tips.

www.hillspet.com: Hills dog foods offers information about their products.

www.iams.com: Iams dog foods offers information about their products.

www.napcc.aspca.org: This is the National Animal Poison Control Center. The 24-hour phone line is 888-426-4435.

www.offa.org: The Orthopedic Foundation for Animals (OFA) maintains a registry of dogs' records regarding elbow and hip dysplasia.

www.pogopet.com: This site offers a variety of health-related articles and features.

www.vet.purdue.edu/~yshen/cerf.html: The Canine Eye Registration Foundation (CERF) maintains a registry of dogs whose eyes have been examined by a licensed canine ophthalmologist.

www.vet.upenn.edu/pennhip/: PennHip maintains a registry of dogs who have been examined for elbow and hip dysplasia.

Dog Training and Behavior

www.apdt.com: The Association of Pet Dog Trainers. You can find a local trainer on this site.

www.cappdt.ca: This is the Canadian Association of Professional Pet Dog Trainers.

www.nadoi.org: The National Association of Dog Obedience Instructors can help you find a trainer in your area.

www.north-attleboro.ma.us/government/departments/shelter/crate.html: Provides information on crate training.

Other Resources

www.arba.org: This is the home page for the American Rare Breed Association.

www.canismajor.com: The dog owner's guide has a wide variety of interesting articles.

www.cyberpet.com: Tips on all kinds of issues relating to living with dogs.

www.dog-play.com: Information about dog sports and activities.

www.petfinder.org: Pet Finder helps potential dog owners find the perfect pet.

www.takeyourpet.com: Lists of thousands of pet-friendly lodgings and resources.

www.thedogdaily.com: Regular features on training and activities you can do with your dog, and true tales of canine life.

www.ukcdogs.com: The United Kennel Club is a dog registry much like the AKC, but which recognizes a greater number of breeds.

INDEX

behavior problems *(continued)*
   chewing, 102
   commitment to change requirement,
     97–98
   crate uses, 73–74
   digging, 102–103
   dog abandonment reasons, 2
   exercise considerations, 97
   failed placements, 119
   fearful aggression, 111
   freedom limiting as tool, 99
   health issues, 92
   jumping (on people), 99–100
   leadership issues, 92–93
   mouthing, 103–105
   natural actions for dog, 91–93
   owner(s) as cause, 93–95
   prior treatment compromise, 60
   prior treatment issues, 93–95
   separation anxiety, 99–100
   submissive urination, 79
   temper tantrums, 104
   unwanted chasing, 105
   when to seek professional help, 93
Belgian Malinois, new owner bonding
  considerations, 57
Berger, Mary Ellen, Italian Greyhound Club
  of America Rescue Rep, 29–30
biting
   aggressive dogs, 108
   problem behavior, 103–105
bonding
   activity types, 55–56, 60–61
   defined, 55–56
   family members, 56
   German Shepherd Dog timeline, 48
   household rules, 58
   leadership issues, 57–58
   new home adjustment timeline, 50–51
   one-person dog reasons, 56
   personality quirk identification, 56
   prior treatment issues, 58–60
   reaction recognition, 56
   time requirements, 55, 57
BONE (Beardies or Neardies), Bearded
  Collie, 13
boredom, problem behavior reason, 95–96
Bouvier des Flandres, new owner bonding
  considerations, 57
bowls, food/water, 43

Boxers
   new owner bonding considerations, 57
   protective attitude, 107
breeders, spay/neuter program as abandoned
  animal reduction method, 5–6
breed experts, rescue group role, 9–10
breeding, mixed breed versus purebred
  statistics, 3
breeds, selection guidelines, 19–22
Bulldog Club of America Rescue Program,
  9, 109

car rides, bonding activity, 60
cats (other pets), new dog introduction,
  66–68
chasing, problem behavior, 105
chewing, problem behavior, 102
children
   bonding time requirements, 56
   frightening activity avoidance, 67
   household rules, 52–54
   humane education importance, 5
   new dog introduction, 47–48
collars
   anti-bark, 101
   author's recommendations, 44
come command, 85–87
commands
   come, 85–87
   down, 83–84
   down/stay, 112
   heel, 88–90
   housetraining element, 74–75
   leash snap and release technique, 85
   let's go, 89
   quiet, 100–101
   release, 83
   sit, 82–83
   stay, 84–85
   treat uses, 82–90
   using in everyday life, 90
   watch me, 87–88
compromise, prior treatment/behavior
  element, 60
consistency, new dog introduction
  importance, 54
contracts
   rescue group adoptions, 35–36
   SPDR (Seattle Purebred Dog Rescue),
     35–36

shelters
    abandoned dog receptacle, 3–4
    versus rescue adoptions, 7–9
Shetland Sheepdogs, breed characteristics,
    19, 21
Shih Tzus, new owner bonding
    considerations, 57
Siberian Husky, breed characteristics, 23
sighthounds, 20, 22
Simons, Kathy, Australian Shepherd search, 26
sit command, 82–83
skills, volunteers needed, 125–127
snap and release, leash technique, 85
socialization
    aggressive behavior considerations, 115
    bonding element, 56
    frightening activity, 67
    household introduction, 68
    importance of, 62–64
    miscommunication, 65–66
    new location introduction, 63–65
    one-person dog reasons, 56
    other pet introduction, 66–68
    prior treatment issues, 58–60
    puppy growth importance, 59
    when to seek professional help, 66
spay/neuter programs, 5, 114
sporting breeds, breed characteristics, 22
SPDR (Seattle Purebred Dog Rescue),
    all breeds, 11–12, 35–36
squirt bottles, barking behavior uses, 100
stay command, 84–85
submissive urination, reasons for, 79
supplies, new dog requirements, 43–45

temper tantrums, problem behavior, 104
terriers, breed characteristics, 22
toy dogs, breed characteristics, 22
toys, author's recommendations, 44
trainers
    biting behavior help, 93
    questions for, 42
    separation anxiety help, 99
    socialization guidance, 66
training. See also obedience training
    come command, 85–87
    dog ownership element, 17
    down command, 83–84
    down/stay command, 112
    heel command, 88–90

let's go command, 88
release (okay) command, 83
sit command, 82–83
stay command, 84–85
techniques, 80–81
watch me command, 87–88
transportation, volunteer position, 125
treats
    command training uses, 82–90
    crate introduction, 72–73
    new dog introduction, 47–48

undesirable behaviors, prior treatment
    compromise, 60
urination, submissive, 79

veterinarians
    microchips, 44
    pet professional referrals, 42
    questions for, 42
    separation anxiety help, 99
    socialization opportunity, 64
vinegar
    barking behavior uses, 100
    housetraining accident uses, 45
volunteering, rescue groups, 122

walks, bonding activity, 61
watch me command, 87–88
Web sites
    AKC (American Kennel Club), 13
    ARPH (Aussie Rescue & Placement
        Helpline), 12
    Google, 27
    SPDR (Seattle Purebred Dog Rescue),
        11–12
    YGRR (Yankee Golden Retriever
        Rescue), 12
working dogs, breed characteristics, 22

Yankee Golden Retriever Rescue (YGRR),
    9, 12
yards
    dog-proofing, 40–41
    new dog introduction, 68
    socialization opportunity, 65
    space requirement issues, 18
    unwanted digging avoidance, 102–103
Yorkie, food/water bowl considerations, 43